59 MINUTES to a
CALMER
LIFE

PAUL McGEE

Foreword By

ANDY GILBERT

First Published in Great Britain in 2001 by
Go MAD Books
Pocket Gate Farm
Off Breakback Road
Woodhouse Eaves
Leicestershire
LE12 8RS

ISBN 0-9537284-3-9

British Library Cataloguing in Publication Data.
A catalogue record for this book is available from the British Library.

Printed and bound in Great Britain by
Cox & Wyman, Reading

**Go M.A.D.® is a registered trademark of
Career Strategies Limited**

The views expressed in this book are those of the author. The intent is only to offer suggestions of a general nature. People suffering from depression should consult their doctor. For those people already on medication it is also important to consult their doctor before making any changes to their routine. The author and publisher cannot be held responsible or liable for your actions.

ABOUT THE AUTHOR

Paul McGee is an international trainer, coach, author and professional speaker. He combines his background in psychology, with common sense and humour to provide practical insights and ideas to help people and organisations achieve greater success. In this book, Paul draws upon his vast experience working with thousands of people over the last ten years, to discover the keys to a calmer life.

ACKNOWLEDGEMENT

If laughter is 'good medicine' then I must thank Gail, Ken, Paul and Barbie for the copious amounts of medicine they've given me. Hopefully I've given some back in return! Special thanks also go to my family for all their support and particularly to my wife Helen. Helen you've lived with me in the 'dark times' and you realise this book is born from experience. Even when the journey was particularly rough, you've always stood by me and never complained. Enjoy the hammock - you deserve it! Finally, thank you to Andy and all the crew at Career Strategies. Being around you all is always an inspiration, even if your football team is better than mine!

Dedication

To Matthew and Ruth with love

CONTENTS

	Page
Foreword	1
Introduction	5
Stress, Separating The Fact From The Fiction	9
Who's Robbing You Of A Calmer Life?	25
Calmer Strategy One Change Your T-Shirt	45
Calmer Strategy Two Be A Coach Not A Critic	63
Calmer Strategy Three E + R = O	75
Calmer Strategy Four Communicate Your Needs	93
Calmer Strategy Five Have Realistic Expectations	105
Calmer Strategy Six Be A Problem Solver	119
Calmer Strategy Seven Chill Out And Sweat It Out	131
Calmer Strategy Eight Organise And Prioritise	145
Calmer Strategy Nine Enjoy The Journey	169
Calmer Strategy Ten Action Brings Satisfaction	179

59 Minutes to a Calmer Life

FOREWORD

One of the many great things about this book is that it is written by a realist and a person who practices what he preaches. Someone who has learned from stressful experiences and developed the skills necessary to lead a calmer life. Paul McGee is an inspirational story teller who, like myself, is passionate about helping others to make a difference. He writes in a style that is easy to read and understand. His words also make me smile!

Having known Paul for many years, I remember a conversation with him in 1998 where he commented that he sometimes ended his speeches and training sessions by encouraging participants to "Go MAD". He went on to explain to me that this was an abbreviation for "Make A Difference". At this time, by a great and fortunate coincidence, I was conducting a research study into how individuals applied key success principles in order to make a difference in their life. And so , the name Go MAD was adopted for the development process that resulted from the research findings.

Now, several years later, Go MAD® is a registered trade mark and recognised as a powerful development process, used worldwide by tens of thousands of people to make a measurable difference for themselves and their organisations. Following the success of my book, "Go MAD - The Art of Making A Difference", I decided to publish further books and Paul McGee was an obvious choice for "Go MAD about dealing with stress". But with both of us believing that you get what you focus on, we definately did not want a book containing the word stress in the title!

So here it is. A book for busy people with less than an hour to spare who are seeking practical tips, tools, techniques and maybe a bit of inspiration about developing a calmer life. It is low on theory, high on practicality and I challenge anyone not to find something of value contained within these pages.

You will find ten calmer strategies outlined, together with many words of wisdom and advice. At the end of each chapter there are a series of questions and exercises to reflect upon. Whilst it might be tempting to continue reading, I encourage you to pause and consider your answers - maybe even write them down - before continuing. You will notice a significant difference by doing this. So feel free to write in the book (unless you've borrowed it from a library!), highlight the parts you like, turn corners over and most importantly use it to **help you make a difference**.

Andy Gilbert
Managing Director
Career Strategies Ltd

"It's never too late to be the person you might have been."
George Eliot

"It doesn't matter when you start
as long as you start now."
W Edwards Deming

INTRODUCTION

In 1997 I had what I considered to be a successful year in my business: I surpassed my financial goals; spoke to large audiences in Hong Kong, Singapore and Malaysia; visited Australia; and even managed to squeeze in a two week holiday in the Isle of Wight with my family. But, although I didn't realise it at the time, I was sacrificing my own health and relationships with my family on the so called 'altar of success'. My life was unbalanced. I was suffering pains in my chest, being increasingly less tolerant of my children, working incredibly long hours, communicating less with my wife and suffering disturbed sleep. Would those outside of my home have spotted anything wrong? Probably not. I was Paul McGee the jet setter, the goal getter, popular with clients and in demand as a business speaker and trainer. Incredibly I even ran seminars on how to handle stress! I was considered an expert on the topic and yet was too busy to realise the damaging impact it was having on my life and relationships.

This book has been born out of experience and not purely from my academic background. From these experiences I looked for the most practical and realistic ideas to achieving a calmer life. I say realistic, because for me some pieces of advice seemed less practical than others. Trying to practise yoga in the middle of a busy supermarket whilst shopping with two small children, was always going to be a challenge. I don't deny the benefits of meditation, aromatherapy massages, or listening to the sounds that whales make, but I was looking for answers that tackled my issues at a deeper level and gave me more than just the feeling of temporary relief. For myself, these lessons have taken many years to learn, yet I hope that by reading this book, you will gain insights and ideas that will help prevent you from making some of the mistakes I've made. Are there really quick, easy answers to the challenges we face? The answer is yes. However, changing old patterns of thought and behaviour takes time. So the answers are easy but their application to our lives isn't. Because of this, I have deliberately kept the book concise in the hope that you will endeavour to re-read it sometime in the future. Repetition is the key to learning.

In increasing my own understanding of myself and the subject, I've read countless books, listened to hundreds of hours of audio tapes and interviewed and listened to people from numerous walks of life. My guess is that somewhere in this book, I may use a quote or use an illustration that I have picked up from someone else and not given them the acknowledgement they deserve. This is not intentional and I apologise in advance to those concerned. Please point out my errors and I will be sure to put it right in the next edition! A calmer life is not a destination, it's more the quality of the journey. I hope this book helps your journey.

Paul McGee.

"Maintaining a complicated life style is a great way to avoid changing it."
Elaine St. James

Stress, Separating The Fact From The Fiction

Stress - a modern day phenomenon?

OK let's get the 'technical stuff' dealt with first. I have often heard older people state, "We never had stress in my day." So are they right? No. Since man was around, stress has existed. (Now before women start nodding in agreement, I'm including them in the wider definition of the word 'man'!) Stress is simply the body's response to a perceived threat or danger. Interestingly, whether or not the danger is real or imagined is not the issue. The part of the brain that triggers this stress response, the hypothalamus, cannot tell the difference between a real or a vividly imagined event. Therefore, if we think or imagine we are under threat or danger, our body reacts accordingly. As we shall see later, our thoughts are incredibly powerful and by tackling our thoughts, we will also be tackling our stress.

Stress can be a life saver

This 'stress response' is actually our body's survival mechanism. It helps prepare the body to either tackle the threat (the fight response) or flee from it (the flight response). Our evolutionary ancestors would find this particularly useful when faced by a sabre

9

tooth tiger. Today, however, modern life has helped create a whole wide range of 'threats', real or imagined, that attack not so much our physical well being, but our psychological and emotional well being. Many people, perhaps unwittingly, are allowing a whole host of imaginary troubles to trigger their stress response.

"Psychological stress is as much a function of how we see the world as how the world really is."
Dr. Paul Martin

The Challenges of The 21st Century

So what are some of the challenges we are faced with in this new millennium?

- A global population increase - possibly as much as four billion over the next forty years.
- Environmental pollution.
- The end of the 'job for life' culture.
- Increased traffic - both on the roads and in the skies.
- More uncertainty regarding the future.
- Noise pollution.
- A continuing breakdown in family support systems.
- A bewildering and sometimes confusing explosion of new technology.
- Food scares.

- Demanding targets and league tables as organisations seek to survive and justify their existence.
- Increased and sometimes unrealistic expectations, often fuelled by the media, that encourages people to want more in a faster time.
- A greater emphasis on the rights of the individual and getting their needs met.
- Perhaps most importantly, all the above taking place in a climate of continual change.

Faced with all these challenges it would be rather churlish to state that stress is not a real issue to many millions of people. In fact, it is actually predicted that all the above will continue to increase in the future. So even if we feel able to cope now, there is no guarantee that we will be able to cope in the future. To put it bluntly, we need all the help we can get.

"Actually, today is just a warm up. Tomorrow promises us an even more complex world, a still faster rate of change and - unless we learn to handle life better - more stress than we ever dreamed of. These soon will be remembered as the 'good old days'."
Price Pritchett

Stress And Pressure - What's The Difference?

It seems the byword for any minor irritation, increase of workload, or pressure to perform, is labelled as 'stress' these days. Perhaps, more accurately, what we should really be saying is that we are experiencing 'pressure'. Whether or not we can cope with this pressure, will determine whether we are likely to suffer from the long term negative affects of stress.

Is Pressure A Bad Thing?

Absolutely not. Without pressure or stimulation, life would quickly become boring and unfulfilling. Depression and anxiety would actually be experienced by far more people than it is now. We need a certain amount of pressure or a sense of challenge to get us out of bed in the morning. As human beings, we function at our best when we have opportunities to grow and develop, and not when stuck in a comfort zone that ultimately becomes a rut. A 'stress free' or 'pressure free' life becomes a meaningless life.

Twelve Factors That Determine Your Susceptibility To Pressure.

As individuals we are all different in what we perceive as healthy pressure. Our levels of tolerance to pressure are also different, as are the strategies we use to cope with it. So what factors make people more prone to pressure? Well, here are twelve for starters.

1. Lack of Competence, Knowledge and Experience. This relates to work, or in aspects around the home such as DIY, cooking or child care. The increase of new technology and the dramatic rate of change, actually means that the competence, knowledge and experience of yesterday is no longer sufficient to help us today. Life is becoming a continual learning process and some people are struggling to keep up.

2. Lack of Interest/Enjoyment. If you find both are lacking in either your work or home life, this can lead to feeling stressed. When I started a job in a bank, I quickly realised I had no enjoyment or interest in the job. Some people feel 'stressed out' simply because they are a square peg in a round hole.

3. Lack of Influence. I am reliably informed that after the start of the race, Formula One motor racing drivers experience their greatest levels of stress in the pit stop. Why? Because they are having to rely on

13

others and are no longer in control. In life, if we feel we have little control or influence over a situation (from a train arriving on time, to whether or not the organisation you work for will restructure) we are more prone to pressure. Whether or not we have a certain amount of control or influence is not the issue. The issue is whether we think we have.

4. Different Values. If what we view as important and meaningful to us, is not a view shared by others, this can lead to conflict and a degree of stress. If being on time is very important to you i.e. if you are not five minutes early, you're late; then other people's more casual approach to time keeping can become a major irritation. Likewise, if what other people think of you is high on your values scale (and it would be for most people) then you can become anxious in your attempt to continually live up to other people's expectations.

5. Fatigue. Long hours, long journeys, unhealthy lifestyle, children, can all lead to a feeling of fatigue. When this is the case, your tolerance to stress can be dramatically lowered.

6. Unresolved Domestic Issues. Whether work impacts on your home life or vice versa, unresolved domestic issues (from an unfulfilled sex life to financial worries) can lead to an inability to cope.

7. Culture. British society in particular has a less laid back approach to life and work than some of our cousins in Scandinavia or our Mediterranean neighbours. Likewise, our work culture, especially one that expects excessively long hours to be worked, does little to promote a calmer life.

8. Change. If I asked you to write your name using the opposite hand to which you normally write, the likelihood is that the whole experience would feel uncomfortable and the quality of your handwriting would diminish. (Occasionally some people discover they have been using the wrong hand all these years!) Although people can and do thrive on change, the amount of change we are facing in and outside the workplace, means we are having to use a lot of coping strategies just to keep up with it.

Resisting change is one of the most common causes of stress in the workplace. People waste far more emotional energy desperately hanging on to how they did things in the past, than it would take for them to embrace the changes.

---

9. Volume Of Work. Many organisations, for cost reasons, have now reduced their staffing levels, although the volume of work may actually have increased. And with more and more people taking time off work through stress, this places an even greater demand on those who remain. Also, many households now have two wage earners, meaning there is less time to juggle the demands of running a home and raising a family. If we are lacking in support, or organisation and planning skills, the amount of work can become an unbearable burden.

10. Temperament. Some people are naturally, more laid back in nature than others. Other people seem to be constantly driven to be doing and achieving things. They behave more like 'human doings' than human beings and can generate unnecessary pressure for themselves.

11. Negative Attitude. Where some people see problems, others see opportunities. Where some say, "Every cloud has a silver lining", others say, "Every silver lining has a black cloud!" Some people even if they won the lottery, would probably say, "Just my luck it wasn't the roll-over week!"

Negativity doesn't guarantee stress, but it does increase the chances.

---

12. Our Personality. As we'll see in the next chapter, peoples' personality, which influences our thinking and behaviour, also influences our proneness to pressure.

And now for the bad news ...... there's more than one type of stress!

In my study around this subject I have identified four different types of stress.

1) Situational. A sudden event occurs; a car cuts you up; a dog runs at you; a child runs into the road. In these situations you have no time to decide on your response - it happens automatically. This is your survival mechanism springing into action. This response is normal and natural and only becomes harmful if you are being faced with such situations continually and your body has insufficient time to return to a state of equilibrium. Certain jobs obviously increase the likelihood of such events occurring; the police force; fire fighters, etc. However, with sufficient support and training and by applying the strategies in this book, suffering from long term stress is not inevitable.

2) Anticipatory. Often referred to as worry, although much of what we worry about rarely occurs. This however, does not stop the body from moving into a state of high arousal and releasing various chemicals and hormones into our system. Many people suffer from anxiety due to what Napoleon referred to as, "Mismanaged imagination."

3) Residual. The event has occurred and yet we maintain it's hold on us by continually reliving the experience. The emotions most commonly attached to this include bitterness and anger and may explain why there is now a 20 week course at Leeds University called 'The Forgiveness Project'. It could also explain why some people from the world of psychology and medicine, believe post traumatic stress counselling can do more harm than good by encouraging the patient to relive the experience.

Sometimes it's not good to talk.
Sometimes it's good to move on.

---

4) Chronic. This type of stress is the one we need to be most concerned about. This state occurs when we are feeling continually stressed and unable to cope. Chronic stress leads to depression and long term anxiety and can result in damaging our health with fatal consequences.

When The Pressure's On .... The Signs To Look For

So how can you tell when you are suffering from stress? Periodically noticing the following symptoms of stress, or experiencing them for a brief and limited amount of time, should not cause you too much concern. However, if you notice the symptoms are persisting or occurring with greater regularity, then you need to be aware that your stress problem could have long term damaging affects both physically and psychologically unless dealt with.

Sexual desire decreases dramatically in times of stress.

Beware of the following symptoms:

- Becoming more prone to illness (e.g. a skin disease that flares up, or experiencing frequent headaches.)
- Continual loss of appetite (or eating excessively in order to provide some form of psychological comfort.)
- Increase in 'bad habits' e.g. smoking, alcohol intake.
- Decrease in self-esteem or confidence (which may be reflected in paying less attention to your appearance.)
- An increase in negative thoughts which could lead to mild forms of depression.

19

- Becoming irrational in your thinking and failing to see things in perspective.
- Being more irritable and less tolerant of others.
- Increased sensitivity (what was "water off a ducks back" last week, now carries far greater meaning).
- Sleep patterns alter. Either you fail to get to sleep quickly or you wake up far earlier than normal with the adrenaline pumping, feeling highly alert and immediately thinking about your problem. (You then also worry about your inability to get back to sleep and the possible negative consequences).
- An inability to concentrate. Your mind seems 'fuzzy' and you cannot think straight.
- Becoming indecisive and struggling to make decisions; sometimes over minor issues.
- Being emotional, sometimes crying or becoming tearful for no apparent reason.
- Being overly aggressive or overly passive compared to your normal behaviour.
- Becoming obsessive in your behaviour. Often this occurs due to your need to 'be in control'.
- An inability to laugh or demonstrate love to others.

Any of the above can be indicators that you are moving into the 'stress zone'. The impact on you though, largely depends on how long you stay in this zone.

"If you are consumed by fear and anger and unexpressed emotion, your body will reflect it. The 'disease' of the mind becomes the 'disease' in the body."
Andrew Matthews

Stress and the Quality of Your Life

Some people choose to ignore the warning signs. Like a petrol gauge that indicates empty, it is possible to sustain performance for a short time, even with these signs apparent. But if you continually ignore the signals you are heading for some form of breakdown. For most people, this is the worst case scenario and such occurrences, although increasing, are hopefully still in the minority. So, what about the rest of us? Well we would all benefit from experiencing less of these symptoms and the level of intensity with which we experience them. The emotions associated with stress, anxiety, fear and anger can all hinder the quality of our lives, however infrequently they occur. It is also worth remembering that the effects of our stress invariably impacts the quality of life of those closest to us.

And Now For The Good News.

The rest of this book is devoted to how we can achieve a calmer life. Whilst pressure is inevitable in our modern world, suffering from the long term effects of stress is not. So what's the answer? Actually there isn't one single answer, but a whole host of them. I have called them the 'Calmer Strategies'. It is likely you will use a combination of them depending on the situations you face. The strategies carry no magical formula with them; the key is in using them. A gardener needs a range of tools in order to maintain their garden. Knowing how they work is all well and good, but if they remain in the garden shed, they are of little use. A gardener also needs to know which tool to use for a particular job; after all you don't cut the hedge with a lawn mower. Likewise, as you read about the calmer strategies, you will realise that in certain circumstances some strategies will be more appropriate to use than others.

So What's Next?

Before we explore the 'Calmer Strategies' let's have a brief look at how our personality and the personality of others may contribute to our stress levels. By increasing our understanding in this area, we will gain further insights into why we behave the way we do and what it is about other people that can cause us to pull our hair out!

22

Calmer Reflections

1. Review the list 'Twelve Factors That Determine Your Susceptibility To Pressure'. Which ones can you relate to in particular?

2. How long have these particular factors been an issue for you?

3. What coping strategies are you currently using to handle your pressure situations?

4. Review the list 'When The Pressure's On ..... The Signs To Look For'. Which symptoms can you identify with?

5. What symptoms can you identify in those close to you that indicates that they are under pressure?

Stress, like pain, is a signal that something is wrong. If you listen to the signal, you can learn to fix the problem.

Who's Robbing You Of A Calmer Life?

Self Awareness Leads To Calm

What is it about your personality that causes you to respond to pressure the way you do? What is it about other people and their behaviour that can drive you to distraction? Why do some people possess the uncanny ability to wind you up and frustrate you, and yet they fail to have the same effect on other people? The answer lies in our ability to understand ourselves and others more.

Throughout my work I have come across a number of models and theories which aim to help us do this. Work by Carl Jung and Dr. David Merrill in particular, has proved invaluable to organisations as they seek to develop teams and identify people's strengths and weaknesses. However, rarely have these models been used to help people understand what it is about their personality that can lead to them experiencing stress in their lives.

**The first step to a calmer life
begins with self-knowledge.**

25

There are many factors that shape and influence the kind of person we are today including values, culture and previous experiences. As such, we are all unique from one another. Despite this, however, research tells us that we do share many similarities with other people, particularly in relation to our personality traits. For the purpose of this book, I have developed a quick and easy exercise to help shed some light on the kind of person you are. It is not meant to be seen as a definitive, scientific guide to your personality, but it will provide plenty of food for thought.

Assessing Your Personality

The following exercise lists a number of characteristics and personality traits that have been divided into four sections. Each section contains a list of 10 traits and characteristics for you to assess. Circle a number below each statement which, in your opinion, most accurately describes you, based upon the following scale:

1 = Never like me
2 = Rarely like me
3 = Occasionally like me
4 = Fairly often like me
5 = Very often like me
6 = Extremely like me

In completing this exercise, you are relying on your own view of yourself. For a more rounded picture you may wish to ask a further one or two people who know you well, to complete the exercise on your behalf.

In order to arrive at your total score, simply add together the numbers that you circled. (The maximum score would be 60 i.e. if you circled 6 for each of the 10 statements).

Assessing Your Personality Questionnaire

A   (1 = Never like me   6 = Extremely like me)

1. **Outgoing and enthusiastic**

   1   2   3   4   5   6

2. **Emotional**

   1   2   3   4   5   6

3. **Thrives on recognition**

   1   2   3   4   5   6

4. Spontaneous and impulsive

   1   2   3   4   5   6

5. Disorganised

   1   2   3   4   5   6

6. Lacks concern for detail

   1   2   3   4   5   6

7. Competitive

   1   2   3   4   5   6

8. Intuitive about other people

   1   2   3   4   5   6

9. Enjoys lots of people contact

   1   2   3   4   5   6

10. Bounces from activity to activity

   1   2   3   4   5   6

TOTAL SCORE =

B   (1 = Never like me 6 = Extremely like me)

1. Enjoys helping others

    1   2   3   4   5   6

2. Happy to listen rather than talk

    1   2   3   4   5   6

3. Generally easy going

    1   2   3   4   5   6

4. Lets others take the initiative

    1   2   3   4   5   6

5. Enjoys lots of people contact

    1   2   3   4   5   6

6. Values feelings above facts

    1   2   3   4   5   6

7. Avoids conflict and confrontation

    1   2   3   4   5   6

8. Prefers to follow rather than lead

    1   2   3   4   5   6

9. Struggles to say no to other people

    1   2   3   4   5   6

10. Able to see both sides of an issue

    1   2   3   4   5   6

TOTAL SCORE =

C   (1 = Never like me 6 = Extremely like me)

1. Enjoys being in charge

    1   2   3   4   5   6

2. Decisive

    1   2   3   4   5   6

3. Goal orientated

    1   2   3   4   5   6

4. Lacks patience

    1   2   3   4   5   6

5. Dislikes long term projects

    1   2   3   4   5   6

6. Makes tough demands of themselves

    1   2   3   4   5   6

7. Needs to feel they have achieved things

    1   2   3   4   5   6

8. Task orientated

    1   2   3   4   5   6

9. Responds well to challenges

    1   2   3   4   5   6

10. May appear inconsiderate

    1   2   3   4   5   6

TOTAL SCORE =

D (1 = Never like me 6 = Extremely like me)

1. Steady and deliberate in their approach

   1   2   3   4   5   6

2. Orderly and systematic

   1   2   3   4   5   6

3. Prefers staying in the background

   1   2   3   4   5   6

4. Less distracted or influenced by emotion

   1   2   3   4   5   6

5. Cautious in their approach

   1   2   3   4   5   6

6. Enjoys problem solving

   1   2   3   4   5   6

7. Needs a lot of detail

   1   2   3   4   5   6

8. Has a tendency towards perfectionisim

1   2   3   4   5   6

9. Dislikes ambiguity

1   2   3   4   5   6

10. Hesitant in making decisions

1   2   3   4   5   6

TOTAL SCORE =

You now have a score for each character. The higher the score, the more you identify with the statements included in that section. In order to relate more to the characters, it is useful to give each a name:

        Character A - *Cheerleader*
        Character B - *Carer*
        Character C - *Commander*
        Character D - *Thinker*

The majority of people completing this exercise find that they have two of the characters scoring more highly than the other two. Having established your top two (although some people do score significantly higher in only one character), let's summarise the main traits of each character.

Cheerleaders are generally enthusiastic, out going people who would rarely be accused of 'bottling up' their emotions. They value praise and recognition, although it is important to stress that this does not mean they are dependent on it. Cheerleaders can often be impulsive concerning their opinions and actions, and do not tend to be the most organised of people. (Organisational skills tend to be developed over time as opposed to coming naturally). They enjoy contact with people and have a tendancy to attempt a number of tasks at once, often starting a new task before finishing another one.

Carers tend to be less extrovert than Cheerleaders, although they also enjoy contact with people. They are happy not to be the centre of attention, often preferring to listen rather than talk. Generally, Carers have an easy going approach to life and are comfortable allowing other people to take the initiative in situations. Carers do not like conflict and confrontation and will do their best to avoid it. They enjoy helping others and can struggle at times to say "no" to people's requests. They would rather say "yes" than run the risk of causing offence. They are more inclined to follow than lead and place great emphasis on how they feel about a situation as opposed to focusing on the actual facts.

Commanders are results orientated people who thrive on challenges. Patience is not a virtue that they are blessed with naturally and they have a strong need to feel they are achieving things or making progress in situations. They can have a tendancy to overlook the people issues when a task needs to be completed and active listening is something they have to work on. Commanders tend to be decisive people who feel more at home with taking action than with lots of time taken up with discussion and debate. They make tough demands on themselves and expect others to meet their own high standards.

Thinkers tend to be less extrovert than Commanders and Cheerleaders, and less people orientated than Carers. They prefer to take a more deliberate, logical, structured approach to tackling situations and feel quite comfortable working on their own. Thinkers are less distracted by their feelings when assessing a situation and often require copious amount of detail and facts before making a decision. Planning and organisational skills tend to come more naturally to a Thinker.

Personality As A Stress Factor

Now let's explore how your personality and the personality of other people, as revealed in this exercise, can influence your susceptibility to stress. In doing so we need to appreciate that there are, of course, many other reasons besides personality why we can find people difficult. As you read through the following, it is worth remembering that no one individual is exclusively one character and therefore, some of the examples are extreme case scenarios.

What Robs A Cheerleader Of A Calmer Life?

- They have a tendency to confuse activity with effectiveness, i.e. believing if they are busy, they must be productive.
- Can become frustrated when they don't receive the recognition they believe they deserve.
- Likely to experience setbacks and problems because they spent little time thinking and planning.
- Any task requiring a lot of attention to detail, is likely to see a decrease in levels of calmness!
- Relying on gut feelings about people can result in them adopting unrealistically high expectations that others fail to live up to.
- Their enthusiasm and motivation can decrease if they are required to spend a lot of time working alone.
- Can take setbacks very personally.

A Cheerleader As A Stress Inducer

- They don't always think through consequences of their actions and the impact it may have on others.
- Not great listeners, particularly when they've got an idea or something to say.
- Can accuse others of being negative when in fact the other person may just want more information and details. This can lead to breakdowns in communication.
- May have a great idea - if only they could find the piece of paper they wrote it on!
- Their enthusiasm can at times be overbearing. Conflict can occur when others don't always share their enthusiasm for an idea.
- May struggle to be a team player if they themselves will receive little recognition.
- Their lack of attention to detail will frustrate other people and hinder the success of a task.

What Robs A Carer Of A Calmer Life?

- Their desire to avoid conflict and confrontation means they are more likely to play the role of the martyr.
- In listening to other people, may lack the opportunity to express themselves.
- Can become a person who others dump on.
- Can end up working and living to someone else's

agenda because they don't like to push their own.
- Hate to be viewed as being pushy or, even worse, selfish.
- Less likely to look at the facts of a situation and analyse it - more likely to get emotional and go with their feelings.
- Can struggle in a pressurised environment where results, not people, count.
- Their loyalty can be misguided - may give people too many chances.

A Carer As A Stress Inducer

- They can be frustrating to communicate with as they hope you'll discover the hidden art of mind reading.
- More likely to sulk than actually talk about the issue.
- Could become a passive aggressive, i.e. acts calm externally, whilst boiling up inside. Then snaps, usually over something trivial when you least expect it.
- Their easy going nature can give the impression that they're not concerned. Their behaviour seems to lend weight to the phrase "If you can keep your head whilst those around you are losing theirs, then you clearly don't appreciate the seriousness of the situation!"
- Often likes to know about you and asks seemingly trivial questions rather than focus on the task at hand. Likely to ask the firefighter, "How was your

journey?" whilst the building blazes around them!
• More likely to hint and suggest, "Possibly, perhaps, maybe, if it's not too much trouble, would you mind at some stage taking your foot off my neck?" rather than spell out what they really want.

What Robs A Commander Of A Calmer Life?

• A sometimes perceived uncaring attitude to people can rob them of the support of others.
• Can become quite anxious and irritable when they feel they have little control or influence.
• Can find it difficult to switch off. Often has to work at relaxing.
• A failure to see quick wins and instant results, leads to discouragement and dissatisfaction. Struggles at times to be at peace with themselves unless they feel they have achieved.
• Can be so focused that they fail to see the big picture.
• Gets easily wound up by people who they perceive as dithering or indecisive.
• Can become quickly bored and demotivated if they lack a challenge.

A Commander As A Stress Inducer

• Can seem to be only bothered about getting a result or achieving an outcome.

• May fail to understand or appreciate other peoples feelings.

• Impatient with people who seem slow or who need more time to think about things.

• Likely to offend without being aware of having done so. Motivational message from a commander - 'You have the potential not to be a loser!'

• Good at interrupting and not allowing people to vent and express their feelings, as they have usually thought of a solution.

• May have a tendency to take the quickest option rather than taking the time to think through a better option.

• Doesn't always adopt an inclusive approach to decision making. More likely to say, "Here's what we're going to do," rather than, "What do you think?"

What Robs A Thinker Of A Calmer Life?

• Will not like being put on the spot or having to give an instant answer.

• Other people being disorganised and lacking attention to detail.

• Their indecisiveness which results from not wanting to make the wrong decision, means at times they end up making no decision at all.

- Struggles to cope with emotional people. Will also become frustrated when those close to them do not respond or are not convinced by logical argument.
- A tendency to struggle through rather than ask for help, means they miss out on the support and advice of others.
- Being the centre of attention for much of the time will prove to be a less than enjoyable experience.

A Thinker As A Stress Inducer

- Their attention to detail, particularly to what is perceived as unnecessary detail, can infuriate people!
- As they are less likely to express outwardly strong emotions, they can be perceived as uninterested and lacking enthusiasm.
- Constant questions particularly to a Cheerleader, will be perceived as negative and putting a dampener on things.
- An unwillingness to make a decision or take action, will frustrate others.
- Their focus on the task and over reliance on logic can alienate the more people orientated individuals in the team.

Is Conflict Between Characters Inevitable?

No, not necessarily. There are many *cheerleaders* who work effectively with *thinkers* and equally *commanders* working successfully with *carers*. (This applies equally in and outside the workplace). However, our predominant personality traits perhaps illustrate how the potential for conflict, disagreement and misunderstanding between people can occur. It is also helpful to realise that people we sometimes label as 'difficult' could be more accurately described as 'different'. Achieving a calmer life begins with the realisation that flexibility of behaviour and greater understanding of others is crucial to improving our relationships. Although we all have predominant personality traits, that does not mean we have to allow them to dominate in every situation. Neither is this exercise a convenient excuse for people to say, "I'm stressed because I'm a *thinker* and you're a *carer*." As the rest of this book will explore, the reason we become robbed of a calmer life, has much more to do with us than anyone else. So, whether you're a *cheerleader, carer, commander* or *thinker,* the ten calmer strategies will be of help to you.

Calmer Reflections

1. Having ascertained your predominant personality styles, review the lists, highlighting what robs you of a calmer life. Make note of the two points which you can identify strongly with at present. Look for ideas in this book to help you address these issues.

2. Choose two people with whom you have a close relationship (at work or home). Based on your knowledge of them, which two personality styles are they most like? If they are willing, you could ask them to complete the exercise in order to gain a more accurate picture.

3. Now reflect on the list, highlighting how your predominant personality style can induce stress in others. Which points do you feel currently affect your relationship and communication with these two people.

"Anyone can become angry.
That is easy.
But to be angry with the right person, to
the right degree, at the right time, for the
right purpose and in the right way -
that is not easy."

Aristotle

Calmer Strategy One
Change Your T- Shirt!

Which T-shirt Are You Wearing?

A key reason why people fail to live a calmer life is because, in certain circumstances, they quit taking responsibility for what they do and how they feel. Imagine for a moment that if what people thought about themselves, was emblazoned across a T-shirt that they wore. Some might have the word 'happy' or 'fulfillled' across their chest. People who choose not to take responsibility for their lives or their future might wear a T-shirt with the word 'victim' displayed in large letters.

A Victim In Conversation

Scenario One :

Victim: "I hate my job and I've got an awful boss. I never get any thanks for what I do."

Friend: "So why don't you leave?"

Victim: "Oh no, I couldn't. I mean, what else can I do? I've been there so long. Anyway we need the money."

Friend: "But have you tried - you never know, there could be a job that would suit you down to the ground."

Victim: "Eh..... who would employ me at my age? No, what employers are looking for now are young people who they can train. Anyway it's years since I've been for an interview, I'd go to pieces."

Friend: "When you say your boss is awful, have you tried talking to him?"

Victim: "You don't know my boss. I've tried talking but he just won't listen. No, I've just got to accept this is my lot and grin and bear it."

Scenario Two :

Partner: "Are you OK?"

Victim: "Fine."

Partner: "Are you sure?"

Victim: "Yes I'm sure!" (they start tidying the room in an overtly aggressive manner, avoiding eye contact with their partner at all costs.)

Partner: "Look, if there's a problem, or there's

something needs doing, just tell me."

Victim: "I shouldn't have to tell you!! You can see the house is a tip, the table needs cleaning, the kids need bathing and all you can do is read the bloody newspaper!"

Partner:"OK I'm sorry. Let me bath the kids, you have a rest."

Victim: "Forget it. I'll do it myself like I always do."

Scenario Three :

Friend:"Are you OK? You seem hassled."

Victim: "I am hassled. I've had to take the car in for a service, the lawn needs cutting and I promised I'd take the kids to McDonalds. I'm looking after Jenny's two whilst she's at the dentist. I'm supposed to be at my Mum's in half an hour and I must get something for Brian's tea. Honestly, my feet haven't touched the ground."

Friend:"Well, look can I help?"

Victim: "No, it's OK. Thanks anyway. No, I'll just have to do everything myself. I never get any help from Brian you know."

Friend:"Well couldn't he have taken the car in?"

Victim: "Well I don't like asking. He's got enough on his plate without me hassling him."

Any of these sound familiar?

So why do people wear the victim T-shirt?

1. They believe they have no other choice. "That's just the way it is, there's nothing I can do" is the favourite mantra when people play the victim role. They have an almost fatalistic approach to life and to the inevitability of being the victim and loser.

2. Low self-esteem and poor self-image. Either of these factors can distort our view of how we see a situation. Our esteem and image can be affected by life events and we are perhaps more vulnerable to seeing our esteem or image lowered when we have experienced some major change such as a divorce or redundancy. Such events can knock our self-confidence which in turn affects how we feel and think about ourselves. A feeling of hopelessness or helplessness (which at times is understandable) leads to a resigned inevitability of wearing the victim T-shirt.

3. It's become a habit. Some people have been putting

on the T-shirt so regularly, they now wear it without even being conscious of the fact. It has become an acceptable part of their regular behaviour and they fail to see what other options or choices they have.

4. People enjoy wearing it. Wearing the victim T-shirt for some people brings them many perceived benefits:

• People feel sorry for them and give them more attention.
• It can increase their own feeling of self-importance.
• It is a good excuse for not being able to achieve other things (I would have been able to achieve ...X...... if only .... had been more supportive.)
• They enjoy being the martyr, as it gives their life a sense of meaning and purpose.
• Blaming others also frees them from the responsibility of taking charge of their own life.

5. They've been told to wear it. Some well meaning parents or friends tell the victim when things go wrong, that there's nothing they can do. Perhaps it's God's way of punishing them or simply that these things are just meant to happen. Some people, they are told, are just lucky - and they're not one of them! So they have to wear the victim T-shirt - after all, it was made especially for them!

How do you change your T-Shirt?

1) Take Responsibility For The Choices You Make

It is worth considering that all human behaviour is driven either by:

a) the desire to gain a benefit (e.g. money, wealth, power, pleasure, acceptance etc.)

or

b) avoid pain (e.g. guilt, hassle, prison, job loss etc.)

You have probably heard people say:

"I wish I didn't have to go to work."
"I wish I didn't have to pay my bills."
"I wish I didn't have to clean the house."
"I wish I didn't have to look after the kids."

Yet when faced with the question, "Well why do you?" the response is typically, "Well I've no choice." Here is the issue; we all have a choice. Are there some people who don't go to work, pay their bills, clean their house and don't look after their children? You bet! However, the consequences of not doing these things, may be something we are not prepared to face. So in order to avoid the pain of unemployment, we choose to work; rather than face prison, we pay our bills; rather than live in a slum, we clean our house; and rather than see our children fostered, adopted or in a children's home, we choose to look after them.

So the choices we are making are consistent with our values, and personal and emotional needs.

To further illustrate the point, let me give you an example I heard from my colleague Barry Stiff. Let's suppose I say that I hate having to mow my lawn. What other choices do I have?

i) Pay someone else to do it. Sorry I'm a bit tight with money, I don't want to do that.

ii) Concrete over my garden. Well actually, I like to enjoy my garden, I wouldn't want to concrete it over.

iii) Just allow your grass to grow. No way. What would the neighbours think? I want to have a tidy garden.

iv) Ask a family member or a friend to do it for me as a favour. Well I don't want to impose on anyone else. I don't want to be seen as a burden.

v) Move to a place with no garden. Like I said before, I enjoy my garden.

vi) Lay down artificial grass which doesn't need cutting. No, that would be too expensive and anyway

I enjoy the smell of freshly cut grass.

vii) Buy a sheep or goat. I'm allergic to farm animals. Anyway, it would be too much hassle looking after them.

viii) Well in that case mow your own lawn and stop complaining!

So faced with all the other alternatives, we have made the choice that suits us the most; to cut our lawn. So if we're doing what we have chosen to do why are we moaning so much?

**Acting like a victim
seriously threatens your future.**

A Friend's Dilemma

Brian, a friend of mine, often complained about spending Christmas with his in-laws. We discussed his range of options and why he was not taking them.

Option A: Refuse to go. Too much grief from his wife! Coupled with the fact that he would feel guilty.

Option B: Allow his wife and children to go, but he would do his own thing. Out of the question, he wants to be with his family on Christmas day.

Option C: Arrange an alternative..........go abroad for Christmas. Well the in-laws are getting older, he wonders how long they'll be around and he prefers a British Christmas anyway.

Option D: Pay for them to go away. This sounds too expensive and they prefer their home comforts.

Option E: Realise it's just one day a year. Choose to enjoy it because faced with the alternatives, this seems by far the best/easiest option for him.

Brian came to the realisation that by choosing to spend Christmas at his in-laws, he was satisfying his own personal and emotional needs at the time. By taking responsibility for the choice he made, Brian decided to quit playing the role of miserable victim every Christmas. When we decide to take responsibility for our own actions, rather than blaming others, it paves the way for us to find solutions to achieve the life we desire.

"Feeling sorry for yourself and your present condition is not only a waste of energy, but the worst habit you could possibly have."

Dale Carnegie

2) Risk Being Seen As Selfish

Many of us have been brought up to put the needs of others before our own. This is a worthy ideal to live up to. (We'll look at how to deal with people who don't ever attempt to live up to this ideal later.) Such a philosophy and approach to life will have many benefits, however if applied consistently, particularly to people who adopt a different philosophy (e.g. "Look after number one"), then it may begin to rob us of a calmer life and lead to burn out. As we saw from our previous chapter 'carers' are particularly motivated by a need to please and help others. This in itself is fine, but it also needs to be balanced by considering our own needs.

Those that are good at helping others,
often struggle to help themselves.

• *What is driving your need to please others?* Is it low self-esteem; they won't like me unless I do.....? Or perhaps as a 'cheerleader', you sense an opportunity to receive recognition, so end up saying yes when you should be saying no.

Many a long term relationship has been damaged by one partner's inability to say 'no' to the requests of other people outside the relationship.

• *Assess the price of being nice.* I was recently asked to take part in a pantomime that was to be performed for underprivileged children. The person asking me felt my personality and acting ability were just right for a particular part and, after all, it was for a tremendously deserving cause (and they were desperately short of people to ask!) However I knew my work schedule, the amount of time I was spending away from my wife and children and the strain it would put on our relationship if I made such a commitment. Diplomatically I said I was unable to help. Did I feel slightly guilty? Yes, a little. However, the question I felt I should be asking is not what will other people think, but what do I need at this particular time?

• *Practice saying , "NO" sometimes.* Being selfish might mean saying no more often. Neither your employer or your loved ones will benefit in the long term if you keep on saying yes to their requests and the requests of others.

Human beings are by nature, prone to take the path of least resistance. If you have a habit of always saying 'yes' and getting involved in other people's problems, they will always come to you.

---

3) Remember Your Rights

Perhaps one of the most important insights for people who have been wearing a victim T-shirt, is to remember the rights they have as human beings.

As an individual you have the right:

• To set clear boundaries.
• To deal with others without being dependant on them for approval.
• To decline the responsibility for other people's problems.
• To make mistakes, because you are not perfect.
• To say 'no' to requests without feeling guilty or selfish.
• To ask for thinking time.
• To have your ideas and opinions listened to, taken seriously and accepted as valid for you.
• To have needs and wants, which may be different from other peoples and to ask (not demand) that others respond to these needs and wants.
• To be treated with respect as an equal human being who may choose to be different from what others would like you to be.
• To chose not to assert yourself e.g. to choose not to raise a particular issue.

4) Remember Your Responsibilities

People often feel happy to declare their rights, but then overlook their responsibilities. If we ignore our responsibilities we may achieve a degree of calmness for ourselves but, at the same time, increase the stress levels of others. I believe passionately that a calmer life should not be achieved at the expense of others. This being the case, we need to be aware of the following responsibilites:

I have the responsibility:

- To accept that other people have their own opinions, feelings, views and ideas, which may be different from my own.
- To talk in a clear way to others so they understand my needs.
- To listen actively in some circumstances to others even when I do not agree with them.
- To accept the consequences of my actions and decisions. Particularly when I choose not to assert myself.
- To acknowledge that other people may choose not to be involved in resolving my problems.
- To learn from my mistakes.
- To acknowledge that others may choose to be different from how I would like them to be.
- To recognise I have a responsibility to others rather than being responsible for others (the exception

being if I have children.)
• To ensure I do not make unreasonable demands of others in order to alleviate my own stress.
• To regularly reflect on my own actions.

"Don't go around saying the world owes you a living.
The world owes you nothing. It was here first."
Mark Twain

---

5) *Quit Always Playing The Rescuer*

It is important to realise that if we are to experience a calmer life, we need to stop believing that we alone are responsible for resolving other people's problems. In an effort to help a colleague, a friend or loved one, we can end up creating a calmer life for them and a more hassled one for us! It can also cause a dependency on us to develop if done consistently; with some people adopting an attitude (admittedly not always overtly so) of, **'What are you going to do about my problem?'** Mothers especially have this habit of continually rescuing their children and failing to make them accountable for their own actions. (OK fathers may also do this but, in my experience, less so than mothers). Now when the child is born, I have no problem with this approach - indeed I think it is highly commendable, up until a certain age! But there does come a time when I believe we should start to make our children more accountable for their actions.

At work, managers can become a dumping ground for their staff's problems with the simple comment, "OK leave it with me." I appreciate helping others can be completely appropriate and, indeed, something to be admired. But it can also be driven by a need for self-importance or for a feeling of being indispensable.

**Helping others can be
driven by our own insecurity.**

When you keep on rescuing people, they will fail to develop their own problem solving skills, and can become dependant on you, resenting it when you are unable to help.

6) If You Are Not Prepared To Do Something - Stop Complaining

I come across in life, people who I affectionately call BMW's. They spend their lives Bitching, Moaning and Whinging! Now I appreciate that some people are only happy when they are miserable and you tend to find they are well balanced people - they have a chip on both shoulders! I am quite prepared to listen to people vent for a while and even more so when they talk about what they are going to do about their problems. But I've made a pact with myself and I apply it to others also.

If you are going to hold a pity party, make sure it's a short one and limit the number of people you invite.

Since I have started to take my own advice, I'm living a calmer and more enjoyable life. I have stopped getting angry about things I cannot change and decided my BMW sessions will be as short as possible. Who needs this victim T-shirt anyway?

When you take off your victim T-shirt and take responsibility for your actions and the situations you are in; you will begin to experience greater peace and start focusing on solutions not excuses.

Don't count on any knight in shining armour coming along to relieve your stress. If you want a calmer life, that is your choice. You can do something to achieve it, but you must look to yourself for the solutions. From now on, how about wearing a T-shirt which has emblazoned across it, *"I am responsible."*

Calmer Reflections

1. On what occasions do you feel you may have worn the victim T-shirt?

2. What caused you to wear the victim T-shirt (we identified five in this chapter)?

3. Review the lists 'Remember Your Rights' and 'Remember Your Responsibilities'. Choose two statements from each list, which are particularly meaningful for you.

4. Are there people who you live and/or work with who are wearing the victim T-shirt? In what ways may you be able to help them? (Lending them this book may be a start.)

Calmer Strategy Two
Be A Coach Not A Critic

It's Your Thoughts That Count

I came across a poster recently, that claimed we have 50,000 thoughts a day. How you can measure this and what the calculation is based on, I am not sure. Whatever the number, my experience and research has shown that the single most influential force that controls our emotions are the silent conversations we repeat over and over again inside our head. Try being negative without having negative thoughts. Try being angry without having angry thoughts. It can't be done. Our thinking affects how we see and feel about life.

**Thinking is a bit like breathing.
Most of the time, we're not conscious we're doing it.**

Ralph Waldo Emerson, in the following quote, succinctly illustrated how the quality of our lives can be the direct result of the quality of our thinking. (If you are not convinced of the validity of this statement, read about the lives of Christopher Reeve or Stephen Hawkins.)

63

"Sow a thought and you reap an act;
Sow an act and you reap a habit;
Sow a habit and you reap a character;
Sow a character and you reap a destiny."
Emerson

How Thought Patterns Can Destroy Your Peace Of Mind

Most people do not consciously decide what to think about. Our thoughts seem to happen automatically, simply popping into our head. These automatic thoughts, which can lead to lengthy conversations with ourselves, can be influenced by a range of factors. The weather, the day of the week, something we saw or heard on the news, our current circumstances, our previous experiences and our culture can all be allowed to influence our thinking.

The reality for some people is that the negative emotions associated with stress, fear, anxiety and anger can all be created inside our own heads. And as we look to the outside world for someone to blame for the stress in our lives, we ignore the single biggest cause - ourselves!

As human beings we quickly develop patterns of

thinking which become automatic and deeply ingrained. These thought patterns can be helpful, but they can be equally destructive. Let's explore four particularly unhelpful patterns of thinking.

1. Inner Critic

This is the inner voice which will come out with statements such as:
"I can't believe you just did that."
"Honestly I'm hopeless."
"Paul you're so stupid."
"I've been a right pillock."
"I never get this right, what's wrong with me."
"My Dad was right, I'll never be good at ...."
"Why can't I be more like my brother/sister."
"I hate myself sometimes."

The impact of these statements is influenced by the intensity and the tone in which they're said, and also their regularity. The Inner Critic has a tone which is both demeaning and demanding. The former professional footballer, Tony Cascarino, in his autobiography gives his own definition of the Inner Critic.

"For as long as I can remember, there has been a little voice in my head that highlights my weaknesses and undermines my confidence."

The Inner Critic can erode your confidence and feelings of self-belief. A lack of these, can rob you of the inner strength and resolve to tackle your problems.

There is no law against beating yourself up internally; yet by doing so, you're probably guilty of grievous emotional harm.

---

2. The Broken Record

It is good to talk about your problems (one of the later strategies looks at the importance of this). But sometimes we can get stuck in the groove, constantly repeating over and over again, the same issues that concern us. This may be appropriate and natural, for instance when you have suffered a bereavement, but some people do this over much lesser matters.

It is OK to vent.
But remember to set a time limit!

Now if we come across a sympathetic 'Carer', they can actually make things worse. Sometimes, being a good listener can result in people reliving the experience and re-awakening their previous emotions. That can have some benefit if people are then prepared to move on, but for some it seems to make the problem worse. The broken record needs little encouragement. A few comments such as, "That's awful," or, "You must feel terrible," will normally suffice!

Although such comments are said with the best intentions, they can exacerbate the issue and give further justification for the broken record to continue to complain about their situation rather than do something about it.

There comes a point when, for our own sake, we need to let go and move on. You cannot manage history. You cannot afford to be a broken record all of the time. You'll lose friends and you'll lose the opportunity to achieve a calmer life.

3. The Martyr Syndrome

The mindset of the martyr is something we explored in Calmer Strategy One - 'Change Your T-Shirt'. Their thinking encourages them to believe they are a victim. They have no choices. Everyone else is to blame for their problems. Such a frame of mind robs them of the opportunity of taking responsibility and finding solutions for themselves.

4. Trivial Pursuits

A story was once told to me about a tree in a Canadian forest. The forest had all but been destroyed due to an electric storm that was followed weeks later by a hurricane. Only one tree remained standing. This tree though having survived two major threats, was destroyed finally by an army of small beetles.

In life it seems some people cope well with the major things (house move, redundancy, etc.), but can completely over react to more trivial issues. Someone is tailgating you? Big deal. The kids have not made their beds? So? Our reaction to trivial events far outweighs their actual importance and yet we can allow ourselves to move into the stress zone.

**Don't let the beetles get you down.
Turn your melodrama into a mellow-drama.**

Becoming A Coach To Yourself

So how can we overcome these unhelpful forms of thinking? Quite simply we need to re-programme our minds. You and I have developed over the period of our lives, deep ingrained thinking patterns. Imagine for a moment that the thinking part of your brain is like a field of tall grass. By walking from one side of the field to the other, you have created a pathway. The more you walk across this field, the more established this pathway becomes. In the brain, these pathways are referred to as neural pathways. So changing unhelpful thought patterns takes time and effort on our part. You have to work at creating a new pathway across the field. It will not work if you say to yourself, "I won't think that way again". You will. You still need to get across the field which is why we need to replace our unhelpful thinking patterns with more constructive ones. The role of a coach is to help a person improve their performance. By coaching rather than criticising ourselves we can create pathways that lead to a calmer life. In order to do this I have developed a series of questions which serve to overcome unhelpful thinking patterns and create a more positive approach. Together these seven questions serve as an antidote to the 'Inner Critic', the 'Broken Record', the 'Martyr Syndrome' and 'Trivial Pursuits'.

LEARN TO PICK YOURSELF UP......

"I did the best I could at the time.
I've learnt; I'm wiser;
I've moved on."

Unknown

THE SEVEN COACHING QUESTIONS

1. Where is this on a scale of 1-10?

2. How can I influence this situation?

3. How important will this be in 6 months time?

4. Is my response appropriate?

5. What can I learn from this?

6. What will I do different next time?

7. What can I find that's positive in this situation?

Not every question by itself will be appropriate in every situation. But, by using them regularly they can help us achieve different outcomes in our lives and experience different emotions. The key is repetition. We have to create a new pathway where one already exists. This will not occur by reading the questions once and then disregarding them. If this is the case you will quickly find yourself travelling along the same old established pathway, achieving the same outcomes and experiencing the same feelings as you did before.

If you always think as you've always thought, you'll always get what you've always got.

Initially you might find it helpful to memorise these questions or type them out and place them somewhere they will be seen regularly. The power is not in the questions themselves, but in the answers they can provide and the actions they can lead to.

Calmer Reflections

1. Which of the unhelpful thinking patterns did you relate to most?

2. Identify some of the trivial events you over react to.

3. Which of the Seven Coaching Questions do you consciously and regularly already use?

4. Which of the questions will you use regularly from now on? In which situations?

There are only two things not
worth worrying about.
Those things you can't change
and those things you can.

Calmer Strategy Three
E + R = O

What's In An Event?

In the excellent audio programme "Self Esteem and Peak Performance", author and speaker Jack Canfield introduces a concept he calls $E + R = O$. Jack explains it is the Event plus your Response that determines the Outcome. Let me explain what this can mean in reality.

Imagine the scene: your boss has just summoned you and a colleague into his office just before 5 o'clock on a Friday afternoon. They are not happy with the performance of either of you over the last week and tell you so in no uncertain terms. Your boss has a point, which you readily acknowledge, but neither you or your colleague are given any time to put forward your view point. You feel hurt, embarrassed and angry. You both leave your boss's office at the same time and then go your separate ways, at the end of what has been a particularly demanding week. As you walk through reception to the car park, another colleague asks you how your meeting went. You launch into a tirade of abuse aimed mainly at your boss with comments such as, "Unfair", "Who do they think they are?" and, "They're not exactly blameless either."

When making your way home in the car, you drive like a person possessed, as you continue to re-live the meeting with your boss; your anger increases, as do your feelings of injustice. Beware any driver who gets in your way tonight! Although usually a courteous driver, tonight is a completely different matter. Your tolerance level hovers around zero and a few unsuspecting car drivers receive a few hand signals not normally found in the highway code book!

Your partner whilst reading the paper, asks the fateful question, "How was your day?" Their apparent lack of concern for the injustices you believe you have suffered, only goes to add further fuel to your burning anger. Friday night is not a good night. You are unable to concentrate on what you are watching on the television, and passion and intimacy with your partner are completely off the agenda. You struggle to get to sleep that night and wake up on Saturday morning in a foul mood. Your partner, perhaps insensitively, tells you to forget the whole thing; their thoughtless remark meets with a stony silence. The rest of the day does not go well. Shopping on a Saturday is never great at the best of times as far as you are concerned and today seems ten times worse. First there's the issue of parking, then playing 'hunt the basket' outside the supermarket. Then it's those screaming children, whose parents seem totally inept at controlling them. To cap it all, you only want a few items, so obediently take your place in the ten items or less queue, in the hope that at least you shouldn't have to wait for too long. To your utter horror and disgust you notice, after a careful analysis, that the number of items in the shopper's basket in front of you does in fact total eleven! You are seething .... why does this always happen to you? Life is so unfair!

Sunday is spent thinking about your imminent return to work the next day and meeting your boss. Monday arrives and the receptionist asks if you've had a good weekend. You explain that it has been an awful weekend and that your boss is entirely to blame.

"When angry, count to four, when very angry, swear."
Mark Twain

Let's go back for a moment to your colleague who was also in the meeting with your boss. As they left work, they were also asked how the meeting went. Their response included phrases such as, "They're just dumping their stress on to me," and, "Their bark is worse than their bite." Friday night is initially spent talking with their partner about their afternoon meeting and how their boss would never get a job in the diplomatic service. However, after this initial discussion, the comment is made, "Anyway, I'm not going to let some little Hitler ruin my weekend, what do you fancy - a bottle of red or white?" And so begins a much needed and welcomed weekend break.

You Are Free To Choose Your Response

The scenario demonstrates how two people can respond so differently to the same event. The Event plus my Response determines the Outcome. For many years I continually blamed other people for how I felt. I believed other people made me angry, sad or wound me up and I had no choice in the matter. This victim mentality continued until I listened to the audio programme by Jack Canfield. It was then that I realised the following:

**It is not the event, but the meaning
I give the event, that determines
the outcome.**

Unlike Pavlov's dogs, who salivated every time a bell rang because they associated the ringing of the bell with being fed, we can choose our responses to most situations. Admittedly, we do have a self-defence mechanism that is automatically triggered on certain occasions i.e. the fight or flight response; but there will be times when we are experiencing a range of unhelpful emotions and feelings which we can control.

Over half the battle in reducing stress is simply becoming more aware of how you respond to situations.

Interpretation Is Reality

I came across a story recently, told by author and cartoonist Andrew Matthews, which amply demonstrates how it is not the event, but how we see the event that makes the difference.

There was once a farmer who had one son and owned a horse. One day, the farmer's horse ran away and his neighbours came along to console him. "What bad luck your horse has run away," said his neighbours. But the farmer replied, "Who knows if it is good or bad luck." "Of course it's bad luck," said the neighbours. After a week, the farmer's horse returned followed by twenty wild horses. The farmer's neighbours visited and said, "What good luck your horse has returned, and with another twenty." The farmer replied, "Who knows if it is good or bad luck." The next day the farmer's son was riding amongst the wild horses when he fell and broke his leg. "What bad luck," said the neighbours who came to console the farmer. "Who knows if it is good or bad luck," replied the farmer again. "Of course it's bad luck," said the neighbours who were beginning to think the farmer was an old fool. Another week went by and an army came through town. They wanted to enlist all the fit young men to go away and fight in distant lands. The farmer's son with his broken leg was left behind. All the neighbours came to celebrate, saying, "Wasn't it good luck your son broke his leg? Now he can stay behind with you." And the farmer replied, "Who knows if it was good or bad luck."

**"Nothing is good or bad,
but thinking makes it so."
William Shakespeare**

How we see or interpret an event, or the behaviour of another person will determine the emotions we experience. Let's look at some common situations.

Situation 1:

You're travelling down the motorway, when despite the fact that you are driving close to the speed limit, a car tailgates you, flashing it's lights in an effort to get you to move over. You could respond in a number of ways, based upon how you interpret the event. You could respond by refusing to change lanes

80

and deliberately not allowing the car behind to overtake you. This response perhaps is based upon you interpreting the situation as some aggressive driver demanding that you make way for them. Their actions, you might believe, demonstrate a level of arrogance and superiority on their part and are a reflection on you for not driving fast enough. Your response therefore, is based upon a desire for revenge and an unwillingness to allow someone to bully you into complying with their wishes. However, you may have responded differently. You could have thought, "Oh, here's another inadequate person, trying to make themselves feel important. I'm emotionally secure enough not to feel the need to stand my ground, so I'll just pull in." Alternatively, you may have thought, "This person is obviously in a rush, particularly as they seem intent on breaking the speed limit. Maybe it's an emergency situation, a sick child or something. I'll just move aside and hope they get there in time."

Situation 2:

You left a message for someone to call you back at work. Two days later, you still haven't received a call. Your interpretation?

a) The message wasn't passed on.
b) They've obviously been very busy, I'll give them another call.
c) They may have forgotten, well we're only human.

d) I'm not important enough. I am a low priority on their list of people to speak to.

Your interpretation could lead to you either making another call, or simply feeling resentful.

Situation 3:

You have friends round for a meal. The evening went well and they stated you must come over to their place next time. Nearly a year has passed and you have still not been invited back. Your interpretation?

a) They obviously didn't enjoy your company after all. By not inviting you back, they're trying to tell you something.

b) Life has probably been that hectic, that the year has flown by. It's not a question of not wanting you over, simply that they haven't got around to organising a suitable date.

c) They actually feel embarrassed to invite you back. They could never match your culinary skills and their dining room is in such a state at the moment, they rarely feel like entertaining at all.

d) They simply can't remember whose turn it is to entertain. They don't really bother about whose turn it is, but you popped round for a coffee a few weeks ago and never mentioned having a meal together, so what's the big deal?

How you interpret the event, could lead to the ending of a perfectly good friendship.

What's Driving Your Response?

A number of factors influence our response to a situation. They include:

• **Our Values.** These determine what is important to us. A scratch on a car may make one person very angry, whilst someone else sees it as just a scratch on a lump of metal. Likewise, some people see time-keeping as very important, whilst others have a more laid back approach to being on time.

• **Beliefs.** These have been shaped and developed over the years particularly during our childhood. If our belief is that we've always had a short temper and there's nothing that can be done about it, then that will influence our response when we feel angry. Equally, if we believe that people think we're stupid when we do something wrong; this will influence our response when we make a mistake or if someone points out a mistake we've made.

• **Peers.** They can greatly influence our response to an event, either through their encouragement - "I wouldn't let them get away with that if I were you" - or simply by the example they set when responding to a situation.

• **Self-Esteem.** Healthy self-esteem could mean we respond to constructive criticism in a much more positive way, than if our self-esteem is low.

• **Motivation.** Can we be bothered to respond differently to an event? For instance, I have occasionally found my levels of tolerance concerning my children's behaviour whilst shopping, plummeting towards zero. However, imagine if I was approached by someone who promised to pay me one thousand pounds, if I could respond in a calm manner towards my children between then and leaving the shop. Could I do it? Of course I could.

Calm does not mean responding in a laid back fashion and showing no concern, but it does mean responding in a controlled and appropriate manner.

Given sufficient motivation, it's amazing how we can respond differently to situations.

• **Self-awareness**. Perhaps some of us have failed to step back and reflect on our behaviour. Are we happy with the outcomes our responses achieve? Have we reflected on how we might respond differently next time? Are we aware of the impact our responses have on other people? A lack of self-awareness and an unwillingness to reflect on our actions, means we can become locked into a cycle of behaviour, which may or may not help us.

Over half the battle in reducing stress is simply becoming more aware of how you respond to situations.

• **Habits**. The more we respond in a particular way to an event, the sooner that response becomes habitual. The undertaking of the most simple of tasks results in complex electrical activity within the brain. As we saw in our previous strategy, the brain creates a series of neural pathways that quickly become established. What is important to appreciate, is that habits can be broken and new pathways established. So responding regularly in a particular way, does not mean we always have to respond in that fashion.

There is a difference between an instinctive reaction and an habitual response.

How To Stop Overreacting To Events

Let us be clear, $E + R = O$ is simply a formula for understanding that the outcomes we experience in life, are not as a result of an event, but due to how we respond to that event. Two people, faced with the same event may respond very differently. In order to live a calmer life, we need to stop trying to focus on changing events and people (which at times will be outside our sphere of influence) and concentrate more on our responses to those events and people. We could get started by asking ourselves three of the questions from our previous strategy 'Be A Coach Not A Critic'.

1. Where is this on a scale of 1 - 10? (If 1 represents of little importance and 10 represents highly important.)

2. How important will this be in six months time?

3. Is my response appropriate?

There may of course be times when the answers to the above questions are: it will still be very important in six months time; it rates as a 9; and my response is entirely appropriate. For example this would especially be the case if I were to discover one of my children was seriously ill or was being bullied at school.

"If I really want to improve my situation,
I can work on the one thing over which
I have control - myself."
Stephen Covey

It is important to realise that the formula $E + R = O$ is not stating that it is wrong to be angry or experience emotions.

Emotions are valid. They need to be
acknowledged not denied. However, the length
of time we experience them and to what
intensity, is to a large extent up to us.

Recognising this to be the case, what else could we do to help ourselves respond more appropriately to situations? Firstly we need to clarify our beliefs and motivation. The following two questions will help us to do that.

1) Do I believe I can respond differently? (Remember the question is not *will* I respond differently, but *do I believe I* can). Asking yourself, "If someone was to pay me a large sum of money to respond differently, could I do so?" - usually helps clarify our beliefs. Most people realise that given sufficient incentive (not necessarily financial) it is possible to respond differently to a situation.

2) Have I a good enough reason why I want to change? This comes down to motivation.

So How Do I Gain Sufficient Motivation To Respond Differently?

The answers to the following questions will help.

1) Is my response to situation X helping or hindering the situation?

2) What would the benefits to me be if I responded differently?

3) Am I both aware and comfortable with how my current responses in situation X are affecting others?

4) Am I achieving a satisfactory outcome for all concerned in situation X, by the way in which I currently respond?

Having clarified whether we believe we can respond differently and are sufficiently motivated to take action, we will be in a much better position to see change occur.

It's our thoughts that make us unhappy and anxious - and we can change our thoughts.

See, Believe, Achieve

The hypothalamus - the part of the brain that triggers the 'stress response' i.e. the fight or flight response - cannot tell the difference between a real or vividly imagined event. Hence your heart can beat faster and your blood pressure rise, simply by thinking about and vividly imagining an event you perceive to be stressful. As Albert Einstein stated, "Imagination is more powerful than knowledge." So how can we utilise this fact to help ourselves? In order to change your response to an event, begin to vividly imagine the event and picture yourself responding in your desired way. Seeing this picture in your mind repeatedly begins to create a different set of neural pathways i.e. a different path across the field. For example, you may imagine yourself dealing with your children or a loved one and rather than responding as you have done previously, you now respond in a calmer way. Actually visualise yourself responding more calmly. This technique applies equally to work situations. Visualise yourself responding effectively and calmly in that team meeting or during that presentation.

Remember, responding calmly does not mean responding passively. You can be both calm and assertive.

Repeating these images over and over again feeds into the subconscious mind and if repeated regularly and with belief, will result in you responding differently. The question is, are you sufficiently motivated to do it?

"Nothing can bring you peace but yourself."
Emerson

The Reality Of E + R = O

Can I honestly say I now always act calmly and appropriately in every situation? The answer is no.

However, where in the past I may have reacted at an eight on a scale of 1 - 10 and remained at that position for a number of hours, I now find myself quickly sliding down the scale and responding in a much calmer way than previously. I still find I will at times become angry and frustrated over minor things, and fatigue particularly reduces my willingness to apply this strategy. The concept is simple, but the application requires work. However, by applying this strategy, the reality is, for me personally, that my anger and frustration is often nipped in the bud and put into perspective. My understanding of $E + R = O$ has enabled me to take responsibility for how I respond to situations. That does not mean I deny my emotions or ignore my feelings. My life would not be as rich, if I did not experience moments of sadness or anger. Likewise, it has not encouraged me to take a passive approach to life. But it has encouraged me to be more creative in how I see an event and more flexible in how I respond. By doing so, I have discovered not just a calmer life, but a more enjoyable life, where my emotional energies are channelled in a more positive and constructive way. Perhaps one of the most invaluable lessons I have learnt is summed up in a quote from Eleanor Roosevelt:

"No one can make you feel inferior without your consent."

Calmer Reflections

1. Identify a time when you became really angry or hurt. On reflection, was your response fully justified? If so, why?

2. What are the issues within you that lead to you feeling so angry or hurt?

3. How long did you remain feeling angry?

4. In what ways could you have responded differently to that situation?

5. Where was the event on a scale of 1 - 10?

6. Where was your response on a scale of 1 - 10? (1 = complete calm, 10 = ballistic)

7. What has been the consequence of your response to that situation?

8. Identify a situation where you wish to respond differently in the future. Visualise yourself responding in a manner that you feel would be more helpful.

Calmer Strategy Four
Communicate Your Needs

The Danger Of The Lone Ranger

It's very difficult to achieve a calmer life by acting independently of others. Whether at work or at home, we all at some time need to interact and be involved with other people. How others behave and communicate towards us, influences our ability to handle situations. A partner who fails to take any responsibility around the house, impacts on the partner that does. The parent who abdicates responsibility for child care, affects the parent who does take responsibility. The boss who fails to offer any support, guidance or praise to their staff, influences the motivation and performance of their team.

An inability or unwillingness on our part to communicate our feelings and our needs can quickly lead to resentment, bitterness and anger. If these feelings are left surpressed and allowed to bubble away, people will either eventually explode or simply withdraw from the situation as a way of coping.

Sometimes it's not brave to keep a stiff upper lip - it's downright stupid.

The Dangers Of Aggression

Deciding only to communicate when we have reached breaking point can make the situation worse. When we communicate from a highly charged, emotional state, we are unlikely to be either logical or rational. (Indeed, the event that triggered off such a reaction may by itself, be embarrassingly trivial in nature e.g. a child's untidy bedroom or a harmless remark from a colleague). Our aggressive approach may in turn provoke an equally aggressive response. When this occurs, a great deal of hurt and pain can be caused and, in some cases, the damage may never be repaired.

If you strike whilst the iron is hot, people usually end up getting burnt. Don't try and resolve conflict with those you care about when you are in an intensely angry state. First of all create some 'space time'.

The Dangers Of Denial

Likewise, it can be equally harmful to deny our feelings or simply ignore them. Such an approach may lead people to view themselves as the victim. In order to cope, they may seek comfort from someone else outside of the relationship in an attempt to raise their self-esteem. Other people will turn to alcohol in an attempt to block out the problem or as a way of coping. Neither approach seeks to address the issue.

"To feel and express anger healthily
is actually the antithesis of madness."
Theodore Rubin

Why Don't We Communicate Our Needs?

Some people believe they shouldn't have to communicate their needs, particularly at home. A common phrase used by some couples is, "But I shouldn't have to tell you." Now why shouldn't you have to tell me? Am I a mind reader? Am I supposed to go around constantly thinking about you and your needs? (If your answer to those questions is, "Yes," then you are in for a huge disappointment.)

'Thoughtful men are the exception that prove the rule'

OK, men can be thoughtful occasionally - usually when there's some pay-back for them e.g. avoidance of guilt or hassle, or perhaps some possible pleasure (usually physical) to be gained. Personally I don't believe men go out of their way to be thoughtless, it just comes naturally! It probably also has more to do with the differences in how men and women think and behave. (For more information on this fascinating subject, get a copy of the Allan and Barbara Pease book 'Why Men Don't Listen and Women Can't Read Maps' or John Gray's book 'Men are from Mars, Women are from Venus.')

In a work context, employees may feel it is a weakness to admit they have needs or are struggling to cope. Rather than admit these needs, staff may take what they see as the easier option and start to take time off work. For some people (particularly if they are a strong 'carer') their reason for failing to express their needs is due to an unwillingness to cause offence or find themselves in a conflict situation.

It is very tempting to raid your museum of hurts when communicating your needs.
Don't - stick to the issues at hand.

The Danger Of Assuming

Whatever the cause, the worst assumption anyone should ever make is that other people fully understand their needs at any given moment in time. Helen, (my wife) and I have had our occasional disagreements; usually stemming from the fact that one of us assumed the other was a mind reader. Perhaps the best piece of advice I ever gave my wife (and I say this in all humility) was, "Treat me like a thick ignorant male and you won't go far wrong."

It is also worth considering the following:

1. We receive the behaviour we are willing to tolerate.

2. Our silence, denial or avoidance gives approval to the situation.

How To Communicate Your Needs

Firstly we need to ask ourselves, "Where is this issue on a scale of 1-10?" If it's not very high, then we may simply choose to ignore the issue or to respond differently. However, when we rate the issue as particularly important, we need to address it. To not do so would damage our chances of a calmer life. When you have decided to communicate your needs, remember it is better to do so when you've had an opportunity to calm down.

**You are more likely to be listened to
if you can communicate in a calm
and controlled manner.**

If you communicate aggressively, you immediately put the other person on to the defensive and they are less likely to listen with a desire to understand you.

The DESAD approach.

One of our biggest challenges when communicating our needs is becoming side tracked and focusing the blame on others. I use an approach which helps both parties stay focused on the issues and work towards a solution. **DESAD** is an acronym I use to describe each stage of the communication process in this particular context. It stands for the following:

Describe the situation.
Explain how and why this situation is affecting you.
Seek solutions.
Agree actions.
Decide on the need to review.

Lets explore each stage in more detail.

Describe the situation. What's concerning you? Have some facts and examples. Describe how the situation is now and how you would like it to be.

Explain how and why this situation is affecting you the way it is. Perhaps you are under performing at work due to a lack of training, or are suffering from stress due to a lack of resources. Maybe your partner needs to realise that you are feeling undervalued due to a lack of appreciation.

Seek solutions. Perhaps the other person can suggest a solution or maybe you have some of your own. It is important to move on to this stage and not to spend too much time looking for all the causes and reasons for why the problem exists. Rather than looking for a scapegoat, look for a solution.

Agree actions. Sometimes we discuss solutions without agreeing how to implement them. What is the first step for you and for the other people involved? Although the discussion of an issue is useful by itself, it is important to agree either how the situation can be resolved or prevented from occurring again.

Decide whether this meeting needs to be reviewed or not (particularly in relation to actions taken) and when this should take place. This initiative would be more appropriate in a work situation, and you may also wish to follow up with an e-mail or note to confirm the actions agreed.

Such a structured approach may, I realise, seem too formal or clinical to use outside the work environment. However, the **DESAD** approach can be used formally or informally and serves above all as a useful template to keep the discussion on track. It can also help you clarify your own thoughts before discussing them. The danger of such conversations without this approach is that you can get things off your chest, but still fail to resolve the issue. Likewise, the person listening to you may perceive you to be simply moaning or nagging, particularly if you fail to explain how and why the situation affects you the way it does.

Communicating Without Blame

Our goal in communicating with the other party is to fix the problem and not to fix the blame. The **DESAD** process will help you to do this. In addition it is helpful to remember the following:

When you communicate, take ownership for your response. For example, saying, "You make me angry," automatically places the blame onto the other person. It is much more helpful to say, "I get angry when........." In this statement you are taking responsibility and ownership for your feelings. Another phrase I have found useful is .... "I realise that might not have been your intention, but the impact upon me was........." Rather than accusing the other party, you are simply expressing the impact their actions have made. Your communication is free from blame yet still clearly lays out your feelings. Having expressed your needs, it is important to also allow the other party to express theirs.

Be Aware Of The Beach Ball

Communication can be a mindfield. Egos, emotions and personalities can create an explosive cocktail. I often use an illustration regarding a beach ball in my courses and seminars. I ask delegates to imagine a huge multicoloured beach ball that reaches the ceiling, in the centre of the room. I make the point that if I were to ask those sitting on one side of the room, what colour is the beach ball, they may answer red, white and blue. However, the people on the other side of the room may answer, orange, green and purple. Now they would both be right; they are just seeing things from a different perspective: Communicating your needs is not about having to prove you are right and the other person is wrong.

101

It is about letting people know how things look from your side of the beach ball.

Helping Others Communicate Their Needs

In my management training I always encourage those present, to ask their staff two questions on a regular basis:

1. **What am I doing that's helping you?**
2. **What am I doing that's hindering you?**

If managers asked those questions regularly, they would have a clearer understanding of how they may be able to help their staff tackle their source of pressure. It's not exactly rocket science, but how often does it occur? And with an increasing number of claims being made against employers by their staff regarding stress related illness, surely this approach is vital for both parties.

However sometimes the tables can be turned:

"**What staff fail to appreciate is, just because I'm a manager, it doesn't make me immune to stress. I find handling change difficult and, if I'm honest, the biggest cause of stress in my life is my staff.**"
Linda, Civil Servant

I have sympathy for some managers. Their case is rarely heard and an inability to deal with a member of staff can be seen as a sign of weakness on their part. Those in a more senior position need to realise everyone throughout the organisation can need support at times, whatever their position. That support often needs to be expressed not in offering solutions, but offering a listening ear. We all have a need to vent at times and being allowed to do so can prove invaluable. As the B.T. advert put it, "It's good to talk." Well, it's also good to listen.

"If I could wave a magic wand and give managers any ability, I would give them the ability to listen. Most managers are good at talking, but effective communication requires both."
Sir John Harvey-Jones

The art of listening is not solely the domain of managers though. It is a skill that could help your partner, help your child, help a friend, help a colleague. It's not always important to have the answers, but it is important to give people time to talk. Used properly, this skill often enables people to discover their own answers.

Calmer Reflections

1. How easy do you find it to communicate your needs?

2. What is your usual way of dealing with an issue that is causing you concern?

3. How helpful has this strategy proved?

4. Identify the people in your life (at home or at work) who you feel you need to communicate more clearly to.

5. What issues would you like to address with them?

6. Are you aware of how things are from their side of the beach ball?

7. How important will this issue be in six months time if it is not resolved?

8. Is there anyone in your life (at home or at work) who you feel would benefit from being encouraged to communicate their needs?

Calmer Strategy Five
Have Realistic Expectations

The Perfect World

Wouldn't it be great to reach our destination on time without any delays? Wouldn't it be wonderful to eat what we want, take little or no exercise and yet have the perfect body? And wouldn't life be just perfect if everyone you came across thought and behaved like you did?

It might be wonderful to think these things, but the reality is somewhat different. Yet despite knowing intellectually that life can be unfair and things can and do go wrong, people still seem to have incredibly unrealistic expectations of life and other people.

There's a huge difference between being optimistic and believing everything will always work out exactly as you planned.

Realistic Expectations Explained

'Realistic' does not mean expect the worst to happen or that we have low expectations of ourselves or others. Neither is it a passive acceptance of whatever comes our way. However, it is an acceptance (not an expectation) that not every situation will work out as we planned and that people (including ourselves) will not always behave or perform in a way we would desire.

Having realistic expectations does not prevent us from communicating our needs or expressing our disappointments. However by adopting a more realistic view of life, we will find that situations and people that have previously caused us frustration, tension and anxiety, are now less likely to do so.

I have found that the less rules I have about how life *ought* to be and how people *ought* to behave, the easier it becomes to live a calmer life. (For example, I used to believe that life *ought* to be fair, people *ought* to be courteous, show me appreciation, be more considerate, etc. When this didn't occur I became increasingly frustrated and unhappy.)

**If happiness for you means everything must go just as you planned.........
I guarantee you will be unhappy.**

Where To Apply Your Realistic Expectations

Let's explore five aspects of life which, due to our unrealistic expectations, can lead to us feeling frustrated, tense and agitated.

1. Be Realistic About Other People.

People are not perfect; they do silly things; make mistakes; break promises; forget to say thank you. That's reality. That doesn't mean we have to sit back passively resigned to such a fact. But it does mean we have to accept that such behaviour occurs.

Yorkshire people have a saying that, "There's nowt as strange or queer as folk." In my experience, that's perfectly true. People have different personalities (don't expect a 'Thinker' to show the same degree of outward enthusiasm for your idea as a 'Cheerleader'.) We also have different values. I would like all road users to be as courteous as I am, but quite frankly they are not! For some people not to return a call or send a thank you note would be unforgivable; but to someone else it's no big deal.

In the area of work, some people may have less of a desire and ambition to achieve than perhaps you do. They are quite happy to do what's required at work, but come home time, that's exactly where they're heading - home. Your priorities in life or at work will be different to others. When you get a clash of priorities, values or personalities, it will inevitably lead to conflict. To expect that we can sail through life without conflict and misunderstanding occurring, is both unrealistic and naive.

Conflict and misunderstanding with people is inevitable. Rather than trying to avoid it, or being surprised when it occurs, we should be looking for ways to handle it.

If you want a calmer life, differentiate between the type of people you come across, those you know well and those who are strangers who you are unlikely to meet again.

If and when conflict occurs with people you do know, much of the advice in Calmer Strategy Four, ('Communicate Your Needs') will be appropriate. But what about that ignorant individual with whom you have a brief encounter? Forget them.

Don't waste your emotional energy getting angry
with strangers you'll never meet again.
Pity them or laugh at them. But save your anger
for something more worthwhile.

---

2. Be Realistic About Travelling

"The traffic was horrendous."
"I can't believe the train was 40 minutes late."
"Our flight was delayed by over 2 hours due to some
   industrial action by the baggage handlers."
"The traffic on Friday evenings is a nightmare."

Delays are inevitable. The amount of traffic on the
roads and the number of people travelling generally is
on the increase. If you build it into your
expectations that such delays are bound to occur at
times, then you're more likely to respond in a calmer
manner when they do. Many instances of road or
general travel rage come as a result of people failing
to have realistic expectations. Perhaps it's because we
take so many things in life for granted, such as
travelling, that we become stressed when things don't
always go according to plan.

3. Be Realistic About Queuing and Waiting

With a global population of over six billion people, you're going to spend some of your life in a queue! And yes, having chosen which queue to join, there is the likelihood that the queue you didn't join will move faster!

The amount of time some people spend trying to find the correct amount of money to pay for their shopping, is in direct proportion to the length of the queue forming behind them.

Some people fail to learn from previous experiences. Going to the doctor or dentist invariably involves having to wait around. Yet how often do you hear people complaining about having to wait, as if it is some strange phenomenon that has never occurred before? When you have more realistic expectations concerning the inevitability of waiting, you can be more proactive. Take a book or magazine with you when visiting the doctor or dentist and if you are seen promptly then that's a bonus.

Here's the good news. Supermarkets, banks, travel agents, traffic lights, airports, etc. are not conspiring against you! It's not personal. It's reality. So get used to it.

4. Be Realistic About Children

Okay you can skip this section if you don't have any kids of your own, never intend having any, and spend your life avoiding places where kids are likely to be found. If not, then read on.

Ed Asner (don't worry, I don't know who he is either) said, "Having kids is part joy and part guerrilla warfare." Well I can relate to that! Yet I've realised that what has contributed to my stress levels has been my own unrealistic expectations of how children should behave. I am not suggesting we accept misbehaviour, rioting or similar misdemeanours; but that we adopt a greater sense of realism to our approach to children. I understand a child's brain is not fully formed until the age of four and yet we often expect children from an early age to fully conform to our standards of behaviour.

Most of what we label as 'naughty' is actually the child acting 'naturally'. Children bicker; siblings are competitive; toddlers find it alien to share toys; and babies seem to instinctively know the inconvenient moment to fill their nappy or practise vomiting skills! Welcome to the world of child care!

Asking a toddler to sit still is like asking a fish not to swim.

Children do misbehave, and some do it deliberately, perhaps in order to gain attention. But often, our reaction has more to do with what's going on in our world than it does with their behaviour.

Often, fatigue, being disorganised, an inability to prioritise, or failing to communicate our needs, is at the root of our stress and not our children's behaviour. For instance, mental and physical fatigue can lead to us saying and doing stupid things.

When we stop making our children solely responsible for our stress and start to have realistic (remember, realistic does not mean low) expectations of them, we move towards a calmer life.

---

5. Be Realistic About Ourselves

I recently came across a case where a girl was diagnosed with anorexia. What's strange about that? The girl was only seven years old! Increasingly, from an early age, people allow themselves to be pressurised by the media and other sources, and develop unrealistic expectations of what they can achieve and what they are capable of.

> "Only a mediocre person
> is always at their best."
> W. Somerset Maugham

Beware The Daily Bombardment

It seems to me that we live in a culture where many people are encouraged to expect maximum results for minimum effort. We are faced with a continual bombardment of messages that I realise are intended to help us, (although in some cases, seduce us) but which can lead to feelings of failures and guilt when guaranteed success does not occur.

- 'You too can have the perfect body in less than 30 days.'
- 'How to become the perfect parent.'

- 'How to stop guilt forever.'
- 'Seven easy steps to success.'
- 'Get rich without working.'
- 'How to never feel unhappy again.'
- 'How to become an overnight success.'
- 'How to become a super parent and still have a successful career.'
- 'Five quick steps to beat stress forever.'
- 'How to feel great whatever the circumstances.'

In order to overcome this bombardment which can make a calmer life seem like a distant dream, we need to subscribe to a charter of realistic expectations regarding ourselves.

"He who begins too much
accomplishes little."
German Proverb

MY REALISTIC EXPECTATIONS CHARTER

1. I will make mistakes sometimes. There's nothing wrong with making mistakes, as no one is perfect. Mistakes can be great teachers as long as I learn from them.

2. It's OK to feel low sometimes for no apparent reason. When things are not going well, it's OK to feel the temporary emotions of sadness, frustration or even anger. In fact it is unrealistic for me to feel positive when I'm feeling emotionally wrung out. I need to acknowledge my pain, frustration and hurt and not deny it. I then need to deal with it.

3. It's alright to fall out occasionally with my loved ones. My relationships will not always be perfect. To never experience conflict or disagreement with others would be unnatural and unhealthy for me.

4. It's normal for me to sometimes feel inadequate as a parent. To sometimes wish I hadn't done or said the things I did. To wish occasionally for 'me times' and to put myself first. It's good for me to realise that the children are resilient and that the bust up I had with them does not equate to me being a bad parent.

5. I accept responsibility for my health and fitness and recognise it's importance. I also acknowledge that my body is not perfect. Genetically, I realise some people will never be super slim no matter how much they try. I accept how good camera work can make people who are in the spotlight perhaps look more attractive than they actually are. I understand that some people have or make the time to become incredibly fit and slim, sometimes at the expense of other areas of their lives. I acknowledge the media's obsession with how people look and how shallow and superficial this can be. I realise that on my death bed, whether or not I have a washboard stomach or cellulite will be irrelevant.

6. I acknowledge I cannot please everybody all of the time.

7. I ackowledge that not everything I want to achieve can be achieved immediately and that it can take years of hard work to achieve success. Therefore I acknowledge the need to set goals, plans and priorities.

8. I acknowledge I need variety in my life. Sometimes challenge and stimulation, sometimes periods of rest and relaxation.

9. I recognise that in order to achieve a calmer life I need to focus on progress not perfection.

10. I acknowledge I can feel comfortable with who I am today, yet still choose to make changes for the better.

Calmer Reflections

1. In which of the five areas explored do you need to have more realistic expectations?

2. Why do you think you have developed unrealistic expectations in this area of your life?

3. What steps do you need to take in order to achieve a calmer life in this area?

4. Which statement from 'My Realistic Expectations Charter' was most pertinent to you? Why was this the case?

Calmer Strategy Six
Be A Problem Solver

Why Do We Worry?

"If worry solved problems, I'd worry." said one of my delegates recently. Some people would argue that it is part of a persons psychological make-up and that people can be 'born worriers'. In some cases it seems to have become a habit which they feel they have no control over. Maybe their parents were unhelpful role models in this area. Some people even mistakenly believe that worrying about something actually helps the situation. It doesn't.

Worry enables you to do nothing except experience greater levels of anxiety.

The Oxford Encyclopaedic English Dictionary defines 'worry' as:

'To allow one's mind to dwell on difficulty or troubles.'

When we worry we become emotionally aroused and are likely to visualise failure or the worst case scenario. This will lead to a state of anxiety which does little to help us apply logic to a given situation or problem.

Emotions can hijack the problem solving skills of the higher brain.

We can't stop worrying about a situation, yet seem unable to actually do anything about it. Excessive worry can lead to feelings of fear and a high state of anxiety. Fear can paralyse you.

"For peace of mind we need to resign as general manager of the universe."
Larry Eisenberg

Let's face facts: the feelings of anxiety and discomfort many of us experience, surround events that will never occur. Our 'mismanaged imagination' robs us of a calmer life.

120

"I've suffered a great many catastrophes in my life. Most of them never happened."
Will Rogers

From Worry To Calm

It is not wrong to experience feelings of anxiety. It is completely understandable to be concerned about a loved one, a child or whether or not you will still be in work this time next year. The realities of life are such that things don't always turn out as we would want. Loved ones become sick, children hurt themselves and people lose their jobs. To be concerned though, is to acknowledge such events may occur, but then we need to concentrate on how to either prevent them or resolve them.

To stop worrying is not an invitation to abandon your responsibilities or to fail to face up to reality.

Change your focus from 'worry' to 'concern'. To be concerned means to be involved, to be aware of problems and to focus on solutions. Think about the word 'worry' for a moment. It is an emotive word. It conjures up negative images; feelings of helplessness. By changing the choice of words you use to describe your feelings, you can change your perceptions of a situation. When something concerns you, ask yourself the questions we have explored previously:

- How can I influence this situation?
- Where is this on a scale of 1 - 10?
- Is my response appropriate?
- How important will this be in six months time?

These questions can automatically help you put the event into perspective and your focus becomes one of dealing with the problem rather than worrying about it. The questions may also reveal that there is very little you can do to influence the situation. If that's the case, why worry about things you cannot change?

Becoming A Problem Solver

When faced with problems at work, many people have little difficulty in applying logic and creativity to resolving them (e.g. how can we improve performance, reduce costs, serve customers better, etc.) However, it seems for some people that's exactly where those skills remain - at work. Areas outside of work, for example, a relationship issue, a child's behaviour, or some domestic conflict, seem to rely more on our emotional response in tackling the situation. It's time to apply some logic to our lives.

Don't curse the darkness light a candle.
Chinese proverb

A method I have used is to ask myself the following problem solving questions:

1. What exactly is my problem?
2. What are the causes?
3. What are the possible solutions? (this could include involving other people.)
4. What are the best/most realistic solutions?

Notice none of these questions asks, "Who's to blame?"

Blaming others fails to help you resolve problems. It might make you feel good that you yourself are not to blame, but it does little to help your situation. When you focus on blame, you focus on the past. You fail to move forward.

Recently I realised I was becoming increasingly anxious when working away in Southend (I've got nothing against the place I promise!). So I applied the four questions.

Q. **What exactly is my problem?**

A. I'm feeling anxious about travelling to Southend. I am unable to relax on Sunday morning when I know I will be travelling away in the afternoon.

"It isn't that they can't see the solution.
It is that they can't see the problem."
Grover Cleveland

Q. **What are the causes?**

A. Travelling by train, then tube, then train and finally taxi in order to complete my journey gives me less feelings of being in control. Even if I get all my connections and everything is on time, my journey will still take five hours. What if the train is late or overcrowded? I also dislike travelling by tube when carrying lots of luggage. What if I can't get a taxi? Will the taxi arrive on time in the morning to take me to my course?

"Take away the cause and the effect ceases."
Miguel De Cervantes

Q. What are the possible solutions?

A. Any of the following:

• Don't take the work in Southend.
• State you are not available on Mondays, then you can enjoy your weekend at home.
• Travel first class. The train might still be late, but it's less likely to be crowded in that section.
• Pre-book your ticket to be guaranteed a seat.
• Take a taxi across London rather than the tube.
• Have the telephone number of two taxi firms, just in case one lets you down. Always book the taxi ten minutes earlier than you require it.
• Forget the train and drive down.

Q. What are the best/most realistic solutions?

A. I now drive to Southend and ideally aim not to

book a training course for Mondays. I still might be delayed (after all I have realistic expectations), however I feel much more in control.

On reflection, the solution to my problem seemed quite straight forward. But then it often does in hindsight. However, the solution was only reached because rather than simply 'feel my problem' i.e. worry, I chose to analyse it instead.

Further Tips To Conquer Worry

1. Write your problem down on paper. Seeing your problem on paper rather than churning it over continually in your mind, can give you a sense of greater control, clarity and perspective.

2. Break your problem down into manageable chunks. Remember the old joke: 'How do you eat an elephant? One bite at a time.' (No I didn't laugh when I heard that either!) Problems broken down become less formidable. Rather than becoming overawed with the size of the problem, this approach brings a greater sense of perspective. (Writing a book can seem like a huge task, but aiming to write just one chapter at a time seems much less daunting.)

Now here's an optimist..........

"When things are bad, we take comfort in the thought that they could always be worse.

And when they are, we find hope in the thought that things are so bad they have to get better."

Malcolm S. Forbes

3. Walk away from your problem. No I am not advocating denial or abdication. However, sometimes we need to allow our subconscious mind time to work on the issue. Have you ever found a solution to a problem whilst doing something else? Suddenly you receive a flash of inspiration even when you weren't thinking about the problem. That is your subconscious mind at work. Walking away from the problem can also help us relax as we are putting less stress on ourselves to come up with an instant answer. Too much pressure can cause the mind to go blank.

4. Take action. There does come a point when we could become caught in 'paralysis by analysis' i.e. over analysing our problem, but doing little about it. We cannot always know for sure whether the action we're taking will be the right one (and yes I know the 'Thinkers' amongst us hate to be wrong), but there does come a point when we must do something. It's much easier to steer a moving car. As the American motivational speaker, Zig Ziglar puts it so well:

"Go as far as you can and when you get there you'll see further."

---

5. Distract yourself. Worry and anxiety can be due to having to wait for a particular outcome e.g. job interview, exam result, etc. As our mind can only hold one thought at a time, we can help ourselves by finding something to busy our minds with. When people ask me whether I'm worried about something going wrong with our house move, I reply that I'm not too concerned, after all, I'm too busy writing this book! Will this approach completely take your mind off your issue? Not entirely, but it does help bring a greater sense of perspective by lessening the chance of unbalanced focus.

6. Change your focus. Remember, worry means to allow one's mind to dwell on difficulties or troubles. What we choose to focus on is up to us. But.........

What you focus on magnifies.

Focusing on the negative can lead us to seeing things completely out of proportion. As Sir Winston Churchill said, "Let our advance worrying become advance thinking and planning." To grasp a calmer life we need to focus on our own sphere of influence and concentrate on finding solutions.

It is possible to break the worry habit, but it takes time and effort to do so. It is well worth it. Doing so can help you bear the fruit of a calmer life, and that is peace of mind.

Calmer Reflections

1. How would you describe the difference between 'being worried' and 'being concerned'?

2. Identify a specific situation in your life where you can apply the four problem solving questions. What insights does the process provide?

3. From the list of 'further tips to conquer worry' which would be the most appropriate for you to do now?

Calmer Strategy Seven
Chill Out And Sweat It Out

Couch Potatoes Of The World Unite

In the age of labour saving devices (remember what life was like before they invented remote controls?) our daily routines are providing us with less and less opportunity for physical exercise. Of course after a hard day at work, a battle home through rush hour traffic, followed by a heavy meal and a glass of wine to help us relax, few of us then feel inclined to embark upon any form of exercise. Modern day society, which seems to place more and more people in front of a computer screen or behind the wheel of a car, has failed to create an environment where fitness abounds. Increased traffic and pollution have meant that you are more likely to ride a stationary bike than a real one and despite a greater interest in fitness, there is little to suggest that people as a whole are getting any fitter.

Your body tackles stress much better when it's got the energy to do so.

Can Exercise Actually Cause Stress?

Actually it can. There will be a few individuals who can become obsessive about exercise (however if it wasn't exercise, it would be something else) and others who cause themselves damage due to their unrealistic expectations of what they can achieve. But to use these examples as reasons why exercise should be avoided is simply propaganda from 'The Couch Potato League'!

So What Is The Benefit Of Exercise?

Quite a lot actually. Here's a few to get you started.

* Improves blood flow to the brain, which can help boost concentration and alertness.
* Lowers blood pressure.
* Can reduce the risk of blood clots.
* Reduces the risk of diabetes.
* Helps prevent weight gain.
* Improves the quality of sleep.
* Raises the endorphin production in your brain. (Endorphins are chemicals in the brain that can give you feelings of well being and contentment.)
* Lowers the risk of heart attacks and strokes.
* Helps burn off adrenaline. (Too much adrenaline can actually lead to us physically shaking.)
* Can help raise our self-esteem.

Feeling fit can make you feel better about yourself and more able to handle pressure.

Although exercise can lead to weight loss, it is important to realise that being physically fit, does not necessarily equate to a sylph-like body. However, taking some form of physical exercise also provides you with the necessary energy required to tackle the challenges of life. Feeling that you are not in control is one of the major reasons for experiencing stress. Exercise gives you the opportunity to take some form of control.

Exercise increases 'alpha waves' - electrical brain patterns associated with calmness.

Struggling To Find The Time?

OK, humour me for a moment. You have just been told that six weeks from now you will die unless you exercise three times a week for around 30 minutes a time. Would you find the time? My guess is you would. It's a question of having a big enough reason why you need to exercise; making it a priority and then scheduling it into your current life style. Time is not the real issue; motivation is.

The amount of time a person spends watching their favourite 'soap' each week on television (1$^{1}/_{2}$ - 2 hours), is equivalent to the amount of time needed to exercise.

But I Hate Gyms

Taking physical exercise does not necessarily equate to going to the gym. Find something (or perhaps discover something) you enjoy doing. Even walking (although you need to do it fast enough and for long enough to increase your heart rate) can prove to have great benefits.

"I realised I needed more exercise -
so now I walk to the chip shop."
David, 43 year old accountant.

What About Sex?

Sex at one level is simply a form of physical exercise during which you burn off calories. (Now you know why some people are slimmer than others!) Perhaps more importantly though, it can provide an opportunity for intimacy. The whole act of love making can prove to be, at least sometimes, both pleasurable and ultimately relaxing. (If this is not the case, you perhaps need to reflect upon one of the previous 'calmer strategies' *'have realistic expectations'*, *'communicate your needs'*, or *'be a coach not a critic!'*) Likewise, if you're struggling to find time for moments of intimacy, then you might need to apply a strategy we'll explore next; prioritise and organise. On occasions we need to create the mood rather than waiting for the mood to occur.

Exercise Realistic Expectations

If you believe there's no gain without pain, you're wrong. Experiencing pain usually has more to do with not warming up or cooling down properly. You are not training to be an Olympic athlete; your aim is to gradually build up your levels of fitness which will in turn help you achieve a calmer life. Any amount of exercise is better than nothing. Consider this:

Long term chronic stress turns the blood to sludge. The fat released into our blood in order to give us more energy, needs to be burnt off.

It's time to stop making excuses and get your kit on (or perhaps in some forms of physical exercise, get your kit off!)

Relax, It's Time To Chill

Right, so having looked at the importance of exercise, now let's examine the equally important area of relaxation. It will probably not come as any surprise to learn that the opposite of the stress response is the relaxation response. Relaxing is essential if we are to lead a calmer life. However, relaxing means different things to different people.

Ten Top Ways To Chill Out

If you're not into yoga or meditation don't worry. Both can prove extremely beneficial in relaxing you, but a calmer life is achieved by finding what works for you. Here is my top ten:

1) Remember The Sound Of Silence. In most typical households today, you are likely to hear the sound of the television, dishwasher, microwave, computer games, phones ringing and people generally yelling their needs. Create some silence in your life. Go for a walk, be with yourself and nature. Don't necessarily think or ponder. Just be.

2) Have A Laugh. It seems laughter really is the best medicine. Scientists at Waterloo University in Ontario, recently established that exposure to humour improves immune system functioning, producing significant rises in the body's natural defences such as

137

antibodies in the bloodstream. Perhaps at times we take ourselves too seriously, which can lead to feelings of stress and anxiety. I now subscribe to 'Joke Of The Day' via the Internet and make sure I include in my diet of films and videos a healthy balance of humour. In the light of all this information, is it any wonder that Britain opened it's doors in 1991 to it's first ever laughter clinic under the auspices of Robert Holden.

Muscles throughout the body tense and relax during laughter, in exactly the same way as with stress reduction techniques such as yoga.

---

3) Watch What You Drink. Be aware of your caffeine intake. Caffeine (which is found not just in tea and coffee, but also in Cola drinks) can produce intense stimulation of the nervous system and actually trigger the stress response. Caffeine also draws the vitamin B out of the body. So if you want to relax more consider reducing your intake of caffeine and drink more water. (The one occasion I would recommend drinking caffeine is when you're driving and feeling tired. In this case, an instant 'pick-me-up' could save your life.)

The first symptom of dehydration is fatigue, not thirst. Drink plenty of water even when you don't feel thirsty.

---

4) **Colour Creates Calm**. Consider the colours in your house and particularly in your work environment. Blue as a colour can help relax people, as can certain shades of green. Other colours such as red and orange, are described by colour therapists as energy colours, fine in certain circumstances, but not in an environment where you want to relax.

Not A Lot Of People Know This But......

Neuropsychologists at the Harvard Medical School, studied longevity and found one clear theme emerged from the contrasting life styles of those who live past 100 - a good sense of humour!

---

5) Practise 7/11 Breathing. Breathe in through the nose to the count of 7 and then breathe out slowly, to the count of 11. Trust me, this will help produce instant calm and can be practised in virtually any situation.

"For fast acting relief, try slowing down."
Lily Tomlin

---

6) Muse To The Music. There's lot's of calming, relaxing music available and music influences our emotions. Whatever your tastes, make sure that if you're feeling stressed, particularly when driving, you listen to music that calms.

7) Have A Sing Song. Singing is one of the fastest ways to change your emotional state. Singing in the shower or in the bath is good for you - and that's official! (In order to reduce the stress in other peoples lives, you may prefer to do this whilst alone!)

8) Scents Make Sense. Certain scents such as pine, lemon or lavender can actually help you relax. Of course it doesn't solve your problems, but may help create an environment where you become relaxed enough to find solutions. Visit a health store or chemist and treat yourself to some calming scents.

9) Pets Promote Peace. I realise that this is not always the case, particularly if you have a young puppy that hasn't been house trained yet, but generally speaking there's something about stroking a cat or dog, or watching fish swim, that's relaxing.

10) Forget Your Focus. In other words, don't allow work to be your sole focus of attention. A great way to do this is to unwind with a book that is not related to work. Likewise, if your work is spent raising your children, make sure you have something non-child related to occupy some of your time. Apart from giving you something to talk about besides children, it also provides an opportunity for you to switch off. An inability to do so, actually increases your chances of becoming stressed. Sometimes, it's healthy to be occasionally distracted, it can help bring a sense of perspective.

"Rest is not idleness and to lie sometimes on the grass on a summers day listening to the murmur of water, or watching the clouds float across the sky, is hardly a waste of time."

Sir John Lubbock

Redefining G.U.I.L.T.

We can all find reasons and excuses for not taking care of ourselves. Sometimes we may just feel guilty when we are considering our needs. However if we intend to live a calmer life, then learning to relax is crucial. Make **G.U.I.L.T.** work positively for you in future by remembering it stands for:

Give yourself

Uninterrupted

Indulgent

Leisure and pleasure

Time at least twice a week!

Calmer Reflections

1. When was the last time you took some form of exercise for over 20 minutes that increased your heart rate?

2. Have you any idea how fit you are?

3. Have you ever considered going to a well woman or a well man clinic?

4. When would be the first/next time you could attend such a clinic?

5. Review the list 'Ten Top Ways To Chill Out'. Identify two that are important for you to either start or continue to do.

"A positive attitude may not solve all your problems, but it will annoy enough people to make it worth the effort."

Anon

Calmer Strategy Eight
Organise And Prioritise

Just Another Perfect Day?

- "There's just simply not enough hours in the day."
- "I must get this report done by Monday."
- "I can't believe I'm running late again."
- "I've got the tea to cook, then get the kids ready for karate, then I must ring Linda tonight......"
- "There's a customer in reception waiting for you, and Taylors rang to say can they bring their meeting forward to Tuesday? Oh and don't forget staff appraisals need completing this week."

The Balancing Act

Life can be hectic. Demands are made upon us not just at work, but at home as well. Everyone plays a number of different roles in life. A typical week will involve me in the roles of administrator, book keeper, gardener, trainer, speaker, chauffeur, cook (occasionally), father, son, husband, brother, mediator (more at home than work), salesperson - the list seems endless. In each role I want to do my best, and yet the demands of one role impact my ability to fulfil the others. Being a father to my two children, who might want to play with me, can become increasingly difficult when I have an urgent proposal to write or a client to visit. So is it realistic to believe, that in the midst of a lifestyle that embraces so many roles and is often lived at a hundred miles an hour, we can ever hope to achieve a calmer life? Well a constant state of peace and tranquillity is probably unrealistic, but a calmer, more balanced, life can be achieved when we learn to prioritise and organise.

Twenty Four Hours Is All We Get

Although we all get the same amount of time each day, how people spend those twenty four hours varies incredibly. My friend Alan is Managing Director of a company, yet still finds time to sit on various committees, run a youth group and support various initiatives at his local church. Claire, meanwhile, does not work. She has two children who are both at school. Yet when speaking to her some months ago about her Christmas preparations, she remarked on how little she had achieved due to never having enough time. Is this really the case or more a question of not being organised?

"It is useless to desire more time if
you are already wasting what little you have."
James Allen

Stress And Time

When we feel we lack control over our time, we can begin to feel stressed. Living life as if it were a constant emergency, robs us of any sense of calm. Yet people will say in their defence, that they simply have no choice - the problem does not lie with them, but is simply an inevitable consequence of living in the 21st century. (OK they may not put it as succinctly as that.) But do we have choices? Is a stressed life inevitable? Is it possible to achieve greater balance in our lives? The answer is yes, but only if we first accept that many of our time problems are due to ourselves.

One of the most valuable lessons I have learnt over the last six years, is the importance of reflection. We all tend to be creatures of habit, and these habits can be a help or a hindrance to us. Reflection gives you the opportunity to consider your patterns of behaviour and to disengage from automatic pilot. To help you do this, here are some questions to answer about time and life management.

"It's become a status symbol in our society - if we're busy, we're important; - if we're not busy, we're almost embarrassed to admit it. Busyness is where we get our security. It is validating, popular and pleasing. It is also a good excuse for not dealing with the important things in our lives."

Stephen Covey

Circle what you believe to be the correct answer.

1. Most people are fully aware of what their main time and life management issues are.
   True / False

2. Time management techniques work well both in the workplace and at home.
   True / False

3. It is always best policy to wait until you have collected and analysed all relevant information before making a decision.
   True / False

4. A job worth doing, is worth doing to perfection.
   True / False

5. In a large proportion of jobs, people use their time in repetitive patterns that can be effectively analysed.
   True / False

6. Frequent interruptions make planning your day pointless.
   True / False

7. Working hard is no substitute for good time management.
   True / False

8. Delegating tasks to other people will always save you time.
   True / False

9. Most of the important results you achieve, stem from only a small number of activities.
   True / False

10. Time management tools will result in you using your time more constructively.
    True / False

11. Having goals helps you to prioritise activities.
    True / False

12. People often fall back into old habits.
    True / False

13. Writing to-do lists are a great way of saving time.
    True / False

14. Time management techniques take away the fun and spontaneity from life.
    True / False

Let's Look At Your Answers

1. Most people are fully aware of what their main time and life management issues are.

The correct answer is **false**. So much of what people do is on automatic pilot, i.e. they do things without consciously thinking about what they are doing. That is why when people are given some straightforward ideas to improve their use of time, they sometimes comment, "Well that's only common sense."

Common sense is only common sense in hindsight.

---

2. Time management techniques work well both in the workplace and at home.

True. The ideas around organising and prioritising are equally valid, in and outside the workplace.

3. It is always best policy to wait until you have collected and analysed all relevant information before making a decision.

False. There will be some exceptions to this of course, e.g. relating perhaps to issues of life and death. But even then surgeons can, and do, take risks when all the full facts are not known. An approach of analysing and collecting **all** relevant information, particularly in an age of information overload, can be an excuse by some people to defer making any decision. Likewise, this indecisiveness (*'Commanders'* would call it dithering) can result in causing stress in others.

4. A job worth doing is worth doing to perfection.

This might be true on occasions, but generally the answer to this statement is **false**. In fact, wanting things to be perfect can raise your own stress levels, which in turn has a knock on effect on others. My friend Colin is a DIY fanatic. But this fanaticism, has lead to his wife saying she would rather pay someone else to carry out the work, because of the amount of frustration and tension it causes within the household. When I recently commented on his newly tiled kitchen, Colin was quick to point out certain faults which he still needed to rectify. He was unable to receive my compliments on his excellent piece of work. Colin felt that until absolute perfection had been achieved, he could not be satisfied.

Continually striving for perfection will lead to ever increasing frustration and anxiety. Strive for excellence not perfection.

---

5. *In a large proportion of jobs, people use their time inrepetitive patterns that can be effectively analysed.*

True. Many people will start to develop routines which can be analysed, even when their job is varied.

6. *Frequent interruptions make planning your day pointless.*

False. Although interruptions are a fact of life (I have received many whilst writing this book), and may lead to you not accomplishing everything you set out to do, they are not an excuse for failing to plan your day.

7. *Working hard is no substitute for good time management.*

True. I have worked incredibly long hours in the past without meeting my objectives. This was due to a lack of planning, preparation, and a failure to prioritise on my part. In Britain, our workforce works longer hours than any other country in the European Union. But this has been no guarantee of success. The cultures of some organisations, has encouraged 'presenteeism', whereby employees feel the need to be present at work for increasingly long hours. However, it is not the length of time you are at work that determines your success, but how you use your time whilst you are there.

8. Delegating tasks to other people will always save you time.

This may be **true** in the long term, but in the short term the answer is probably **false**. Delegation usually requires providing the other person with information and, depending on the task, support and training. Failure to do so, leads to what is commonly referred to as the 'dumping syndrome'.

9. Most of the important results you achieve stem from only a small number of activities.

True. The principal being referred to is the pareto principle or the 80/20 rule, e.g. 80% of your business comes from 20% of your customers. You wear 20% of your clothes 80% of the time, etc.

10. Time management tools will result in you using your time more constructively.

False. Tools are only effective when regularly applied and maintained. Linda, a delegate who I met three years ago, was what can be best described as a seminar junkie. She continued to attend numerous courses and seminars, constantly looking for the magic wand answer to her problems. The answer for Linda lay in applying what she had already learnt.

11. Having goals helps you to prioritise activities.

True. Having goals will help you to prioritise and, on occasions, result in you not carrying out certain tasks because they fail to bring you closer to your goal.

12. People often fall back into old habits.

True. It is believed by some psychologists, that it can take 21 days to form a new habit. Hence, when we behave in a new way, we can, unless disciplined and motivated, quickly fall back into our old patterns of thinking and behaving.

13. Writing to do lists are a great way of saving time..

False. 'To do lists' need to be used correctly. I used to write a 'to do list,' but failed to prioritise the tasks on the list. By doing so I fell into the trap of confusing activity with effectiveness.

14. Time management techniques take away the fun and spontaneity from life.

False. By using your time more effectively, it creates opportunities for more fun and spontaneity. Time management techniques are tools which are there to serve you, not turn you into an inflexible slave to a system.

TIME TO GET
RUTHLESS....

If you haven't worn a certain item of clothing in the last two years, give yourself a further two weeks to do so. If you still don't wear it, then it is time to give it away.

If we are serious about achieving a calmer life, we need to take responsibility and focus on our own sphere of influence in order to make better use of our time.

Ultimately, the quality of our lives is determined by how well we use our time. An inability to organise and prioritise, will cause our stress levels to rise.

Five Tactics To Help Make The Most Of Your Time

Tactic 1 - Set yourself goals and objectives

These can be applied on a daily, weekly and monthly basis. In order to do this, you must consider all your roles in life, particularly those outside of work. (We can very often be clear on our goals at work, but then neglect these principles in our personal life.) Goals help you to establish your priorities. For example, perhaps I had decided it was important to spend time with my children over the weekend because I had been working away from home during the previous week. So if my goal is to spend Saturday with my children, and then I am asked if I want to attend a business event in London on that day, I am in a better position to make a decision based on my goals and priorities.

Where There's A Will

My health is particularly important to me (I previously lost my job when I became ill with M.E.), so I make it a goal to exercise three times a week. Because it is an important and clear goal of mine, my focus is, "How can I make time this week to achieve it." I don't think, "I wonder if I might find time?" However, I need to be organised if I'm going to fulfil my goal, particularly when I spend a great deal of my time travelling. By deciding on your priorities you will find that, whatever your lifestyle, if it's important to you, you **will** find a way to achieve it.

"It's easy to say, "No" when there's
a deeper, "Yes" burning inside."
A. Roger Merrill

Write Down Your Goals

Having a list of vague goals floating around your head is not enough. Each year, my wife and I sit down together to discuss our family goals for the year ahead, and write them down. This includes where to go on holiday; friends to visit; organising a weekend break without the children; what we want to do on the house; etc. It is important to have realistic expectations in regards to what you wish to achieve. Hence, there are some goals which we decide to postpone, either due to a change in priorities, or because aiming to achieve them would cause too much unnecessary pressure.

So why is it necessary to write goals down? Firstly, the very act of writing your goals helps clarify what you wish to achieve. Secondly, writing them down also helps you to see more clearly how one goal in your life, relates to and impacts on other goals. Finally, it is immensely satisfying to review your goals at the end of the day, week, month or year and to assess how much you have achieved.

How Goal Setting Helped Me To A Calmer Life

One goal I have been working on over the last twelve months has been the number of Sundays I spend travelling to my work destination for the following day. Two years ago, 80% of my Sundays involved me travelling away from home. For me, personally, I found that Sundays were no longer a day for relaxation. Now, I am in a fortunate position in that I can decide which days of the week I will be available to conduct my seminars and courses. Because of the goal I set myself, I have now reduced the number of days I am available to work on Mondays. As a result, I have halved the number of days I spend travelling away from home on Sundays. The issue is not whether you have the same amount of freedom as I do to make this particular choice. The issue is, in what areas of your life do you need to set goals? What actions do you need to take in order to reduce your stress and pressure, and improve the quality of your life?

Where there is no vision, the people perish.

The Book Of Proverbs

Tactic 2 - Plan and Prioritise

Having goals helps you to prioritise, because you are able to determine which tasks or requests carry greater importance to you. However, we still need to plan how we will achieve our goals and objectives. At times, we put ourselves under pressure by living as if everything in life is an emergency. Not everything has to be done today. Ask yourself, "When does this need to be completed by?" Then plan your actions accordingly. Perhaps some of those actions need to be built into your daily schedule, whilst others can be built into your weekly or monthly schedule.

Prioritising Activities

This is an approach I use to prioritise my work, although I appreciate it won't be applicable to everyone. I categorise all my post and work into three in-trays:

Intray One - *Important and urgent.* This needs to be looked at and acted upon today. Your goal is to have this intray empty or this particular piece of work done completed by the end of the day.

Intray Two - *Important but less urgent.* You can wait a couple of days before acting on this. But don't ignore this intray for more than two days, otherwise some of it's contents may have become an intray one item!

Intray Three - *Not important (at the moment) and not urgent.* This is the intray for paperwork, tasks, circulars, magazines, etc. that you would like to look at, but know that they are not a priority to act upon at the moment. Sometimes, they may include articles you would like to read, or some information which you need more time to reflect upon. This is the intray to look at with a cup of coffee and a bin close by. Seeing this intray full, should not cause any guilt, but serve as a reminder that it's about time you put aside some time to chill out and wade through!

"There cannot be a crisis next week.
My schedule is already full."
Henry Kissinger

Which ever method you use to prioritise work, the key is to recognise that not all your activities are of equal importance.

Plan Time To Prioritise

As little as five minutes uninterrupted reflection and review time can prevent you using your time inappropriately and enable you plan to and prioritise activities. This quiet time with yourself, is your opportunity to briefly review your daily, weekly, and monthly goals. It could prove to be the most important meeting you attend each day.

A Simple Question To Help You Prioritise

When you have a number of tasks to complete and you are not sure which to do next, ask yourself:

What's

Important

Now?

Tactic 3 - Limit Your Monkey Collection

Kenneth Blanchard in his book, 'The One Minute Manager Meets The Monkey,' describes how managers collect other peoples monkeys, i.e. problems. For example, a member of staff approaches a manager stating that they have a problem. The manager replies using those four immortal words, "Leave it with me!" The manager has now assumed full responsibility for the problem - as the monkey is passed on to them.

This issue is not solely a problem for managers, but for anyone who finds it difficult to say, "No" to other peoples requests or demands. The 'Carers' amongst us are particularly susceptible to this trap. You will begin to notice that people, both in and outside the workplace, can become skilled in dumping their monkey collection on you.

Sometimes the best help you can give someone, is to allow them to help themselves.

Being eager to please and help others is a worthy principle, but be aware you are not the saviour to everyones' problems. Such an approach to life, whilst satisfying at one level, can lead to stress and anxiety at another.

Tactic 4 - De-clutter Your Environment

There is a difference between being organised and organising your clutter. Clothes, toys, books, files, etc. can clutter your home or work environment. If you have moved house or office, you will be aware of the amount of junk human beings have a habit of acquiring. How much time is wasted due to our inability to find things, or space consumed because, "I might want that one day." In 95% of cases, you won't need it at all. Clutter and calm can be uneasy bedfellows, so isn't it about time you paid a visit to the tip or a charity shop?

**Declare one day a year as
National De-clutter Day!**

Tactic 5 - Get Real

Whilst I agree that an optimistic outlook on life is beneficial, I am also aware of how it can lead to unrealistic expectations, in relation to what we can achieve. We have already explored the strategy 'Have Realistic Expectations,' so suffice to say, we sometimes need to be realistic about the time frames we give ourselves to accomplish certain tasks. Unrealistic deadlines lead to increased pressure and, being unrealistic about the amount we can achieve, invariably leads to disappointment.

No Magic Wands

Sadly, there is no magic wand that will eliminate all your time management challenges. Crises will occur; so too will interruptions. Plans will have to change, and circumstances beyond your control will also affect your use of time. However, despite these realities, the strategies explored, when applied, will help you achieve a calmer life.

Calmer Reflections

1. What strategies or tactics do you currently use to organise and prioritise your use of time?

2. Of the 'Five Tactics To Help Make The Most Of Your Time,' which one for you, is the most important to apply?

3. By applying this tactic, what do you believe the benefits to you would be?

4. What, if anything, is preventing you applying this tactic immediately?

Common sense is genius dressed up
in working clothes.

American Proverb

Calmer Strategy Nine
Enjoy The Journey

This is not a dress rehearsal

Imagine the following boxes represent a day of the week:

Now imagine each day of the week represents a decade of your life.

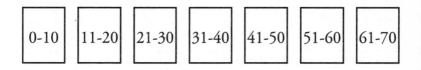

Let's hope we all get a few bank holidays as well! I am aged 36 which, according to this model, puts me on Thursday afternoon. When I considered this fact, I decided some things in life were just not worth getting stressed about. I am no longer prepared to allow a weekend to be ruined over something trivial.

Neither am I prepared to put my life at risk, whilst driving, in order to save a few minutes. I began to ask myself some important questions. How long would I allow the bitterness of the past to rob me of the joy of the moment? How long would it be before I decided to tell someone I loved them, valued them, and needed them? I am now no longer prepared to postpone happiness until I've reached the perfect weight or achieved all I want to in my career.

**A calmer life is not a destination,
it's the quality of the journey.**

I've now realised there is a lot I can do to improve the quality of my journey. It starts by realising that my journey might not be as long as I thought it was going to be. I realise life will continue to throw us challenges, but I believe they can be dealt with more effectively when I decide to enjoy the journey. In our previous Calmer Strategy, *'Organise and Prioritise,'* we explored ideas on how to use our time more constructively. Our aim in exploring, *'Enjoy The Journey,'* is to help us understand why we need to organise, prioritise, and identify the areas of our lives in which we need to apply these ideas.

"Twenty years from now you will be more disappointed by the things that you didn't do, than by the ones you did do. So throw off the bow lines. Sail away from the safe harbour. Catch the trade winds in your sails. Explore. Dream. Discover."
Mark Twain

Defining 'Enjoy'

I am conscious when I use the word 'enjoy,' it can be interpreted in a number of different ways. In the context of achieving a calmer life, let's clarify its meaning:

Enjoy doesn't mean ....

• At the expense of others.
• Avoid tackling important issues or taking personal responsibility.
• Instant gratification and forget the consequences!
• Continual self-centred indulgence.

Enjoy does mean ....

- Creating time for self.
- Spending time with loved ones.
- Having fun.
- Setting and achieving balanced goals.
- Forgiving yourself.
- Forgiving others as best as you are able (for your sake not theirs).
- Forgetting the cost and calories once in a while.
- Getting a buzz from making others happy.
- Enjoying today rather than someday.
- Remembering life is too short for trivial pursuits.
- Taking responsibility.
- Not allowing the past to determine our future.
- Being thankful.

"Enjoy the journey for us means being
able to laze around the house
and keep our nighties on."
Beth aged 7, Annie aged 9

Finding The Balance

A conversation with Peter, a friend of mine, brought home the fact that it is difficult to enjoy the journey when you fail to see the big picture of your life. I had asked Peter what kind of year he'd had.

He explained how he had just completed his most successful financial year yet and had worked in several different countries. He had achieved one of his main goals, which was to purchase a brand new sports car, and had recently acquired a new prestigious client. Yet as Peter told me all this, his facial expression and tone of voice failed to convey any degree of pleasure or satisfaction. I remarked that despite what he was telling me, he didn't look particularly pleased. Peter then went on to explain that over Christmas, his wife had given him an ultimatum. Unless things in their relationship changed, that would be their last Christmas together. He explained how he had fallen into the trap of convincing himself that all his hard work and time away from his wife and young children, was for the good of the family. He now realised that what little time he did spend with them, saw him demonstrating little tolerance or understanding, because he had, in his own eyes, more important things to focus on. His family received the dregs of his understanding, energy, and enthusiasm.

"It is not what we have,
but what we enjoy,
that constitutes abundance."
Anon

Listening to Peter, I realised I had set myself unbalanced goals and that if I didn't make certain changes in my life, then it might not just be Peter who was receiving an ultimatum. The following model, that I developed, has proved invaluable for helping me see the bigger picture and for determining the goals I need to set in each area of my life.

The Life Balance Model

Family Friends	Work Finances
Health Leisure	Personal Development Contribution

Each quadrant is self-explanatory except, perhaps, for Personal Development and Contribution. Personal Development relates to any area of our lives where we wish to increase our learning and understanding.

This development and personal growth can come about through a number of ways, including going to night school, attending a workshop, listening to tapes, reading a book, surfing the web or spending time with other people. It can encompass the mental, spiritual, or emotional areas of our lives and does not necessarily equate to passing an exam or gaining a qualification. Contribution relates more to our giving. This can be in the form of giving our time, talent, or finances for the benefit of others.

**"As long as you live,
keep learning how to live."
Seneca**

Achieving life balance is not about giving equal amounts of time to each area of our life necessarily, but about seeing the danger of paying too much attention to one aspect of our lives, and neglecting the others.

Beware of what you might become
in pursuit of what you want.

What It Means In Practise

Mark, a senior manager in an organisation I work with, explained how at the start of each year, he makes booking holidays and weekends away with his family a priority. Many people can make these family occasions less of a priority, and then struggle to find sufficient time in the year to make such events occur. They then blame the pressure of work, rather than their inability to prioritise. (In some cases I realise work is used as an excuse not to be with the family, perhaps due to relationship difficulties.)

"Success is not about having material things.
Success is more to do with emotional
fulfilment."
Joanna Birch, Marketing Manager

176

The model helps me to reflect on areas of my life which could easily be overlooked. For instance, when was the last time I gave something back to society? My friend Barbara talks enthusiastically of the immense sense of satisfaction and perspective that sponsoring a child in the third world provides. I have also come to realise how my life is not a series of separate compartments, but a series of interconnections. My health affects my ability to work and spending time with family can also be connected with my leisure pursuits (e.g. watching football with my son Matthew). Also, if I fail to develop myself, that is likely to impact on my effectiveness at work. Less work, could lead to less money, which in turn affects the other areas of my life.

In certain cases, the pressures of life arise from focusing too much on leisure activities and not enough on work and what we want to achieve with our future. Wanting life to be all play can place people in a vulnerable position if they have failed to acquire and develop new skills. Some people devote more attention to planning next years holiday, than they do to the rest of their lives.

There's nothing more stressful than being aimless in life. You need to have a sense that you can shape your own future.

Calmer Reflections

1. Which day of the week are you on, in terms of your age?

2. How does that make you feel?

3. What insights does it provide for how you spend the rest of the week i.e. your life?

4. Of those people who are very close to you, which day of the week are they on?

5. How might that influence your interaction with them?

6. Which area of the life balance model do you want to spend more time on?

7. What actions do you need to take in order to achieve the balance you desire? (Remember, have realistic expectations).

8. Review the list 'Enjoy Does Mean.' Identify one statement that is particularly meaningful for you. Why have you chosen that statement above all others?

Calmer Strategy Ten
Action Brings Satisfaction

The Lesson From The Candle

Some years ago, I came across an exercise, whilst working on a training course, which demonstrated why myself and many other people fail to live a calmer life.

Brendan, a colleague I was working with on the course, had been emphasising to the group, the importance of a positive attitude. He stated that people were capable of incredible things, simply by the power of their minds and he was about to demonstrate this fact. He produced a large candle which he placed on a table at the front of the room. He then lit the candle and explained what was going to happen. As a group we were to focus our minds on the candle and *will* the flame to go out. He stressed the importance of being positive and believing it could happen. We all stood up as a group, and the lights in the room were turned off. We focused on the flame. After about thirty seconds I noticed the flame was flickering. Was this actually going to work? As a group we continued to channel our mental energies onto the flame, and Brendan once again reminded us of the power of our minds. Then after two minutes of seeing very little achieved,

Brendan went up to the candle and blew the flame out. He turned to a rather bemused group of people and stated an invaluable lesson. **"Thinking about something is not enough. We need to take action!"**

Putting It Into Practise

We've now explored nine strategies which, when regularly applied, can lead to a calmer life. Each strategy by itself though, might not be enough to reduce your stress and anxiety. In many cases, a combination of the strategies will be needed and, as I have emphasised before, it is important to realise that not every one of them is appropriate for every situation. The key is knowing which strategy to apply in a particular circumstance. To help clarify your understanding and the effectiveness of the strategies, let's explore some questions I'm regularly asked by people when conducting training sessions on the subject of how to achieve a calmer life.

Q. I've got a very difficult and demanding boss. They seem to take out their stress on me. What should I do?

A. Not an easy question. However, a number of strategies may be appropriate. Firstly, you might need to ask yourself how regular a problem is this? Is it happening once a day, once a week, or once a month? What impact is this having 0on you? By answering these questions, you can then best decide which strategy to apply. If this has become a big issue to you then perhaps strategy four *'Communicate Your Needs'* may be most appropriate. If you feel your boss is not prepared to listen, then consider expressing your thoughts in writing. Emphasise that you wish to do a good job, and you empathise with the pressure they are under. However, explain the impact their behaviour is having on you. If you are not prepared to do this, for whatever reason, remember our first strategy *'Change Your T-shirt'*. Do not act as the victim. You do have choices as to how you deal with the situation. Maybe you also need to *'Have Realistic Expectations'*. What do you really mean by 'your boss is difficult?' Do you have an unrealistic expectation of what a relationship between a member of staff and their manager should be like? What you describe as *difficult,* may also be described as *normal* by someone else. It may be worth reflecting on their personality style(*Cheerleader, Carer* etc.) in relation to your own. This may provide you with further insights which help you address the situation. Perhaps it would also be worth reflecting on our third strategy E + R = O. How appropriate is your response to your manager's behaviour? In what ways could you respond differently to the situation? You may feel you are unable or, perhaps more likely, unwilling to influence the situation at work. In that case, you would find strategy seven *'Chill Out And Sweat It Out'* your best action. This will involve you making choices as to what you will do outside the workplace to reduce your levels of stress. For example, you may decide to take some exercise in order to release some of the tension and frustration you are experiencing. The final strategy I would want you to consider is number nine, *'Enjoy The Journey'*. We can spend a considerable amount of time at work, and that time can also influence the quality of our life outside the workplace. You have to ask yourself, how much is my workplace situation affecting the quality of my journey? This will then help you decide what actions you need to take. Remember, we receive the behaviour we are willing to tolerate.

"I just wasn't prepared to put up with the intimidation and the autocratic style from the owners of the business. Quitting a job at my age was no easy decision, but I did so for the sake of my physical and emotional well-being. Three weeks after leaving I landed a wonderful new job."
John aged 54

Q. I'm struggling to combine running a home, raising a family and having a job. I'm constantly tired and have started arguing more with my partner. What can I do?

A. Firstly, have *'Realistic Expectations!'* We can cause ourselves to experience high degrees of stress by the tremendous amount of pressure we place upon ourselves. In this case, a number of strategies would be useful. Strategy six, *'Be A 'Problem Solver'* , would be your starting point. What really are the issues for you? Is it in relation to the expectations you have of yourself? A woman on my course recently stated that despite working full time and having three school aged children, it was still her responsibility to have a meal waiting for her husband when he returned home from work. Perhaps it was not surprising she was on my stress course!

Another action you need to take is to visit a doctor to check on why you are constantly feeling tired. Strategy eight, *'Organise And Prioritise'*, is also crucial when we have a number of roles to juggle. Decide with your *'Realistic Expectations'* hat on, what your goals are for each week. Remember to focus on priorities which may well mean making sure you have at least one family night a week to do something together (besides watching the TV.)

In my experience, people who find themselves struggling to juggle their roles, have usually failed to apply strategy four - *'Communicate Your Needs'*. What could your children do that they are not currently doing to help the situation? Pocket money could be linked to the satisfactory completion of chores. (I appreciate a five year old being asked to carry out essential roof repairs may not be appropriate.) Your partner, likewise, may be able to do a few little things which would actually be a big help to you, which they have never considered doing before. (Putting the toilet seat down for example.) In my experience, we found hiring a cleaner, even for just 2-3 hours a week, made a tremendous difference to us. Time spent cleaning in an evening was now spent on more constructive and pleasurable pursuits.

Because there is rarely one single reason for why we may be struggling to juggle our roles, a combination of strategies will be required. Experiencing instant relief is rare. However, by applying the strategies you will see progress made over time.

Q. Is Christmas inevitably a stressful time?

A. Whether you celebrate Christmas or not, any occasion when people gather together for some form of celebration can be potentially stressful. Strategy eight, *'Organise And Prioritise'*, is very important. For example, if you celebrate Christmas, leaving your shopping until mid to late December will inevitably bring its own pressures. However, people can now shop via the Internet and most, if not all, food stores extend their opening times in the run up to Christmas, with some even open 24 hours. If we are honest with ourselves, something like 'Christmas stress' has more to do with us than it does the actual event.

"Shopping in a deserted supermarket at three o'clock in the morning, four days before Christmas, was one of the most relaxing experiences of the year."
Brian, Senior Manager, British Telecom

You may even decide it is appropriate to re-negotiate who gets cards and presents. A number of people I know only send cards to people they rarely see. Interestingly, they have found those friends that did not receive a card, have *not* decided to terminate their friendship. If you decide you could never do such a thing, remember that is *your* choice. If that is the decision you make then please stop complaining about how stressful an event like Christmas is.

Remember, any celebration which involves entertaining friends and family can also be a source of pressure. This is more likely to be the case when we decide everything has to be perfect for our time together to be a success. It is important to have *'Realistic Expectations'* concerning any special occasion. Children will squabble, batteries will not be included and, inevitably, people will fall out and say things they shouldn't. Celebrate it all and *'Enjoy The Journey!'*

"It will be a very traditional Christmas, with presents, crackers, door slamming and people bursting into tears............"
Victoria Wood - Comedienne

Q. Once I get into my car, I'm a completely different person. I'm like somebody possessed. I've tried being more relaxed, but it doesn't work. Is there any hope?

A. In answering this specific question I will draw upon a number of the insights we have explored in the Strategy **E + R = O**. But first you must answer two important questions.

1. Do you believe you can act in a calmer manner? (Notice I said 'calmer'. It is completely unrealistic and, in fact, dangerous for people to drive in a completely relaxed state all of the time. If you are faced with a dangerous situation, you want to be in a state of high mental alertness.)

186

2. Have you a good enough reason why you want to become a calmer driver?

Let's deal with the first question. I recently worked with Chris, who genuinely believed he would always remain an aggressive driver and could not change. So to my first question, 'Do you believe you can?', he answered "No." I then used a technique, we previously touched upon, which I have found to be extremely powerful. I asked Chris to imagine the following scenario: Imagine there is a camera inside your car that monitors and records your behaviour whilst driving. Let's say you are about to embark upon a journey that will last two hours and will involve some motorway driving. During that journey you will be 'cut up' twice, 'tailgated', come across three sets of road works, and seen one driver queue jump as the motorway went from three lanes of traffic to two. Now imagine how you would normally respond. However on this occasion, you know that your reactions are being recorded. After the journey is complete, three judges will assess your behaviour recorded on film. If, in their opinion, you responded in a concerned but calm way, you will be awarded £5,000. The question is, could you respond in a calmer way?

Chris immediately realised he could respond in a calmer manner given sufficient motivation and as such, his 'beliefs' had been changed.

The second question gets to the heart of what is people's motivation. I have had some people challenge me by saying, "I bet you couldn't get me to change." Actually, they're right, I couldn't. My courses are not designed to prove my ability to change people. My role is to help facilitate that change and I do so by sharing and exploring a range of proven tools and strategies. People have to be open to change and actually *want* to change in order for it to occur. Some delegates have come with a passive approach to learning, believing I will somehow make them into a calmer person. I can only help the process.

When you have answered those two questions, you are then in a position to apply the following:

Firstly, have *Realistic Expectations*. There will, on occasions, be delays to your journey. Accept this might happen, rather than become angry every time it occurs. Some drivers will not be courteous; that is a fact of life, but remember the vast majority probably will be. There will also be that strange breed of driver who hogs the middle lane, oblivious to all that is going on around them. Pity them. Accept that they are probably living in a state of almost total oblivion to most things in life!

Then we need to remember $E + R = O$. Just because you reacted (on a scale of 1 - 10) at an eight, doesn't mean you have to stay there. Remaining angry does nothing to help the situation, in fact it could make things much worse. Why allow the actions of an insignificant stranger to affect your emotions for so long? Remember, they don't care if you are angry or not. Ask yourself, "Where is this on a scale of 1 - 10? Is my response appropriate? How can I influence this situation? How important will this event be in six months time?"

"Resentment or grudges do no harm to the person against whom you hold these feelings. They simply eat away at you."
Norman Vincent-Peale

It will also help if you practise 7/11 breathing. Breathe in to the count of seven and breathe out slowly to the count of eleven. This will have an instant calming effect. (If you find yourself passing out due to a lack of oxygen, you're obviously not doing it correctly!)

You might also want to consider developing a calm drivers mantra. It sounds wacky, but if you seriously want to become a calmer driver, this will help. Start repeating the following phrase, *"I am responding calmly and appropriately when driving."* It doesn't matter if you feel stupid saying it, but bombarding your subconscious mind with this phrase will make a difference. (You need to repeat the phrase a number of times for up to three weeks to really see the difference.)

Finally place somewhere on your dashboard, the following question:

'Is it worth it?'

The answer to that question could actually save your life.

Q. My children drive me mad on occasions. I feel so angry with them sometimes. Then I feel guilty. What can I do?

A. When we explored the strategy *'Have Realistic Expectations'* we briefly looked at this in relation to children. I cannot emphasise enough, how important this strategy is when you are dealing with children. Kids can be draining, not just physically (particularly when they are young) but perhaps even more so emotionally. To feel angry with them at times, is only natural. Let me share a few insights which may help, although for a more in depth look at the subject I would recommend Steve Chalke's book 'How To Succeed As A Parent' and Dr. Christopher Green's two excellent books, 'Toddler Taming' and 'Beyond Toddlerdom'.

It is important to make allowances for tiredness. On a recent shopping trip to a large DIY store, my five year old became almost hysterical when I informed her we would be visiting Burger King and not McDonalds (due to convenience not preference). I do not always respond this way, however, on this occasion I simply hugged her and did my best to reassure her. I quickly realised using reason was not the answer and me shouting at her would only make the situation worse. Within two minutes she was asleep. Adults aren't great to be around when we're tired and children are no exception. However, they are less able to communicate their needs and probably don't always realise themselves why they are feeling lousy. Let's be a bit more understanding of childrens' behaviour when they are tired.

Another way for those dealing with children to achieve a calmer life would be to re-examine the rule book. I have observed that a number of parents make a big deal over a little issue. I am not advocating the abandonment of discipline, however, is it really the end of the world when, for instance, a child has their elbows on the table? I have seen children sent to bed over this issue. We can make life very difficult for ourselves with our uncompromising requests. For example, "You are not leaving the table until you finish all your meal." Compromise should not be seen as a dirty word. Perhaps we should use it a little more as a strategy when dealing with children.

Children need rules and they need discipline. But we need to apply common sense as to which areas we really want to make an issue of. Failure to do so will inevitably result in an increase in our stress levels.

"I can't believe my son's behaviour at the moment. First, he won't eat his carrots and now he's stopped eating the stems off his broccoli."
Yvonne, harassed mother of two

As we have explored previously, a calmer life will remain illusive unless we are prepared to be selfish sometimes. Parents need time and space away from their children. Obviously too much time and space will seriously impact on the quality of our relationships. However, if you want quality time with your children, you also need quality time with yourself and if you have a partner, with them also. Remember, your kids need a break from you as much as you need a break from them on occasions. I love to relax with my children, but I also know that there are times when children and relaxation just do not go together.

Finally, allow children to communicate their needs. My children are only aged five and seven, but I am already realising just how important it is to listen to them. I believe one of the main causes of relationship difficulties between parents and teenagers is due to a parents unwillingness to actively listen. Listening with an 'I know best attitude' is not really listening at all, but just simply waiting for your turn to talk. My children have a right to express how they feel, even if I don't agree with them. There have been occasions when, because I have failed to listen, I have jumped to the wrong conclusion. We can achieve a calmer relationship with our children when we spend time listening to them.

"Being a calmer parent can lead to calmer kids."
Nicky Frisby, parent

These four ideas will not bring about an immediate transformation in your relationship with your children, or bring about a household overflowing with peace and tranquility, but they are a starting point to build upon. By applying these ideas, you are more likely to reduce the amount of stress and tension you are experiencing.

Action Is The Key

Much of what you have read in this book is both obvious and common sense. My aim has not been to provide you, the reader, with gimmicks or novelties, but with practical ideas and insights which, *when applied,* will lead to a calmer life. The challenge, I believe for most of us, is not in aquiring more knowledge, but applying that which we already know.

"Being responsible is to realise our choices are significant - what we do affects who we are and where we will end up.
In short our future is flexible."
Phil Baker

Let's spend some time reviewing the Calmer Strategies, reminding ourselves of the key points from each one and challenging ourselves to take action.

Calmer Strategy One - Change Your T-Shirt

• Choosing to wear the victim T-shirt can make us more prone to pressure because we abdicate our personal responsibility and blame others for our stress.

• We alone are responsible for the choices we make in life. We make our choices based on our values, and our personal and emotional needs.

• In order to alleviate stress, we must at times run the risk of being seen by others as selfish.

• When we do take responsibility for our actions, stop making excuses and avoid blaming others for our stress, we take a vital step to achieving a calmer life. Taking responsibility for where I am now, empowers me to make the necessary changes to achieve a calmer and more fulfilling future. Our world won't change until we do.

What specific action and changes will you make in relation to this Calmer Strategy? (Please write down your answers.)

_____

_____

_____

Calmer Strategy Two - Be A Coach Not a Critic

• The most important conversation you have today will be with yourself. These internal conversations can bring us to a place of calm or into the stress zone.

• We can develop unhelpful thinking patterns that become deeply ingrained. We need to replace the 'Inner Critic', the 'Broken Record', the 'Martyr Syndrome' and 'Trivial Pursuits' by becoming a coach to ourselves:

The Seven coaching questions are:

1. Where is this on a scale of 1-10?
2. How can I influence this situation?
3. How important will this be in six months time?
4. Is my response appropriate?
5. What can I learn from this?
6. What will I do differently next time?
7. What can I find that is positive in this situation?

• We need to ask ourselves these questions regularly if we are to achieve different outcomes in our lives and manage our emotions more effectively.

What specific action and changes will you make in relation to this Calmer Strategy?

Calmer Startegy Three - E + R = O

It is not the event, but the meaning we give the event, that influences our response and leads to a particular outcome.

• If we want to experience different outcomes in our lives, we need to take charge of our responses to events.

• There are a number of factors that can influence our responses, particularly our levels of awareness. Failing to reflect on our actions can result in us being locked into a cycle of thinking and behaviour which may prove to be unhelpful in our endeavour to acquire a calmer life.

• Responding calmly and appropriately does not equate to being weak or passive. You can be both calm and assertive.

What specific action and changes will you make in relation to this Calmer Strategy?

_____

_____

_____

"Men are disturbed not by the things that happen, but by their opinion of the things that happen."

Epictetus
(An Ancient Philosopher, in case you were wondering!)

Calmer Strategy Four - Communicate Your Needs

• Failing to communicate our needs and 'putting on a brave face' can lead to resentment, bitterness and anger on our part - the antithesis of a calmer life.

• Assuming that people will be aware of our needs without us having to communicate them, is naive. People are not mind readers.

• Do not strike whilst the iron is hot, as people usually end up getting burnt. Avoid communication when in an intensely angry state. Allow yourself a cooling off period.

• Stick to specific issues and do not use this opportunity to talk, as a reason to re-visit old issues.

• Remember the beach ball. Communicating your needs is not about proving who is right or wrong, but letting people know how things look from your perspective.

• Others also need to be encouraged to communicate their needs and we can aid this by listening actively.

What specific action and changes will you make in relation to this Calmer Strategy?

_____

_____

_____

Calmer Strategy Five - Have Realistic Expectations

• Having realistic expectations does not mean expecting the worst, or having low expectations of ourselves and other people. However, it is an acceptance (not expectation) that not every situation will work out as planned and that people (including ourselves) will not always behave or perform in a way we would desire.

• By having realistic expectations, we will find that situations and people that have previously caused us frustration, tension and anxiety are now less likely to do so.

• In particular, we need to be realistic about our expectations of other people, travelling, queuing, children and about ourselves.

• Having realistic expectations does not prevent us communicating our needs to others or expressing our disappointments. Neither does it mean we passively accept a particular situation or the behaviour of another person.

What specific action and changes will you make in relation to this Calmer Strategy?

Calmer Strategy Six - Be A Problem Solver

• Worry enables you to do nothing except experience greater levels of anxiety. Worrying about a problem does not help you solve it.

• We are less likely to think logically, the very skill we need when faced with stressful problems - when we worry.

• Much of what we worry about never actually occurs, however, choosing not to worry is not an invitation to abandon your responsibilities or to avoid facing up to reality.

• One method for tackling problems is to answer the following questions:

    1. What exactly is the problem?

    2. What are the causes?

    3. What are the possible solutions?

    4. What is the best/most realistic solution?

• Sometimes it is useful to walk away from our problems and allow our subconscious mind time to work on the issue.

• Remember, what you focus on magnifies. Focus on solutions and not on the problem.

What specific action and changes will you make in relation to this Calmer Strategy?

_____

_____

_____

Calmer Strategy Seven - Chill Out And Sweat It Out

• Modern day living provides us with less opportunities for physical exercise as part of our normal daily routine. Yet the body tackles stress much better when it's got the energy to do so.

• One of the many benefits of exercise is that it raises the endorphin production in your brain. (Endorphins are chemicals that can give you feelings of well being and contentment.) It also increases 'alpha waves' - electrical brain patterns associated with calmness.

• People often use the excuse of not having enough time as the reason for not exercising. However, the real issue is our personal motivation. It's a question of having a big enough reason why you need to exercise.

• Taking physical exercise does not necessarily equate to going to the gym. Find something (or perhaps discover something) you enjoy doing.

• Relaxing is the opposite of the stress response. It is essential to do if we are to lead a calmer life. How you relax is up to you, just make sure you do it.

• If you begin to feel guilty about relaxing, then give guilt a new definition:

Give yourself

Uninterrupted

Indulgent

Leisure and pleasure

Time at least twice a week!

What specific action and changes will you make in relation to this Calmer Strategy?

_____

_____

_____

Calmer Strategy Eight - Organise and Prioritise

• We need to accept that many of our 'time' problems are due to ourselves.

> "It is useless to desire more time if you are already wasting what little you have."
> **James Allen**

• Becoming more effective in your use of time begins with reflection. We all tend to be creatures of habit, and so reflection provides the opportunity to consider our patterns of behaviour and to disengage from automatic pilot.

• Being clear on your goals, both in your personal and professional life, is the starting point from which to organise and prioritise.

• Limit your monkey collection. Beware of unecessarily being drawn into resolving other people's issues and believing yourself to be the saviour to their problems.

• De-clutter your environment. 'Clutter' and 'calm' are

uneasy bedfellows. I believe a minimum of 30% of your possessions could be given away and you would never miss them.

• Do not confuse being busy with being effective in your use of time. Our inability to prioritise and say "no" will lead to a sense of not being in control. This feeling is one of the biggest causes of stress on our lives.

What specific action and changes will you make in relation to this Calmer Strategy?

_____

_____

_____

Calmer Strategy Nine - Enjoy The Journey

• A calmer life is not a destination, it's about the quality of the journey. Your journey should not consist of regretting the past, or worrying about the future. It is about reflecting on your life as a whole and deciding that you are responsible for the quality of it.

• To 'enjoy' means a number of different things. It includes: remembering life is too short for trivial pursuits; spending time with loved ones; not allowing the past to determine the future; forgiving yourself and others; and getting a buzz from making people happy.

• The 'Life Balance Model' helps us to see the bigger picture. It consists of four key areas, any of which when ignored will have a detrimental affect on the quality of your journey. These areas are family and friends, work and finances, health and leisure, and personal development and contribution.

What specific action and changes will you make in relation to this Calmer Strategy?

_____

_____

_____

Calmer Strategy Ten - Action Brings Satisfaction

• A calmer life comes through taking action. That action may involve doing something, or it may involve you giving up something.

• A calmer life is not achieved by simply thinking about making changes.

• The action you take may involve applying a combination of the calmer stategies in order to achieve your desired outcome.

• Things don't change unless you do.

"Do or do not - there is no try."
Yoda (Star Wars)

207

Please write down your top six actions that you will take as a result of reading this book.

1.

2.

3.

4.

5.

6.

And now, stretch yourself by writing three more actions.

1.

2.

3.

And Finally

Having identified your top six actions, you now have a choice. These actions can remain good intentions that are quickly forgotten, or they can be acted upon. Whether your life becomes a calmer one is in your hands.

"An ounce of action is worth more than a ton of theory."
Friedrich Engels

So remember, the key to a calmer life lies not in reading the book or knowing about strategies. Neither does it lie in waiting for the magic wand to appear. It lies in taking action.

The doorway to a calmer life
begins to open the moment you
take action.

Paul McGee provides a wide range of services to organisations and individuals through:

Workshops
Seminars
Speeches
One to One Coaching

For further information you can contact him directly at:

Paul McGee Associates
20 Delphfields Road
Appleton
Warrington
Cheshire
WA4 5BY

www.paulmcgee.com

paul.mcgee2@virgin.net

Contact The Go MAD Team...

If you would like to receive more information about other books in the Go MAD® range, or details of other Go MAD® personal and business development products.

OR

If you are looking for new, inspiring, motivational ways to develop employees through innovative programmes, we offer a range of Go MAD® solutions, which include conference speakers, personal coaches and consultancy.

**Go MAD Ltd
Pocket Gate Farm
Off Breakback Road
Woodhouse Eaves
Leicestershire
LE12 8RS**

01509 891313

www.gomadonline.com

info@gomadonline.com

Other Go MAD® Titles

Go MAD! - The Art of Making A Difference

Contagious Customer Care

Go to Work on your Career

Go MAD About Coaching

If you would like to involve others in achieving a calmer life, visit the website:

www.principlefive.com

On this site, you will be able to electronically network with other people interested in making a difference in all areas of their life.